RELIGIOUS EDUCATION IN THE PRIM

I0571304

Other titles in the Cassell Education series:

P. Ainley: *Young People Leaving Home*

P. Ainley and M. Corney: *Training for the Future: The Rise and Fall of the Manpower Services Commission*

G. Antonouris and J. Wilson: *Equal Opportunities in Schools: New Dimensions in Topic Work*

M. Barber: *Education in the Capital*

L. Bash and D. Coulby: *The Education Reform Act: Competition and Control*

D. E. Bland: *Managing Higher Education*

M. Booth, J. Furlong and M. Wilkin: *Partnership in Initial Teacher Training*

M. Bottery: *The Morality of the School*

G. Claxton: *Being a Teacher: A Positive Approach to Change and Stress*

G. Claxton: *Teaching to Learn: A Direction for Education*

D. Coffey: *Schools and Work: Developments in Vocational Education*

D. Coulby and L. Bash: *Contradiction and Conflict: The 1988 Education Act in Action*

D. Coulby and S. Ward (eds): *The Primary Core National Curriculum*

L. B. Curzon: *Teaching in Further Education* (4th edition)

P. Daunt: *Meeting Disability: A European Response*

J. Freeman: *Gifted Children Growing Up*

J. Lynch: *Education for Citizenship in a Multicultural Society*

J. Nias, G. Southworth and R. Yeomans: *Staff Relationships in the Primary School*

A. Orton: *Learning Mathematics* (2nd edition)

R. Ritchie (ed.): *Profiling in Primary Schools: A Handbook for Teachers*

A. Rogers: *Adults Learning for Development*

B. Spiecker and R. Straughan (eds): *Freedom and Indoctrination in Education: International Perspectives*

A. Stables: *An Approach to English*

R. Straughan: *Beliefs, Behaviour and Education*

M. Styles, E. Bearne and V. Watson (eds): *After Alice: Exploring Children's Literature*

S. Tann: *Developing Language in the Primary Classroom*

H. Thomas: *Education Costs and Performance*

H. Thomas with G. Kirkpatrick and E. Nicholson: *Financial Delegation and the Local Management of Schools*

D. Thyer: *Mathematical Enrichment Exercises: A Teacher's Guide*

D. Thyer and J. Maggs: *Teaching Mathematics to Young Children* (3rd edition)

W. Tulasiewicz and C.-Y. To: *World Religions and Educational Practice*

M. Watts: *The Science of Problem-solving*

M. Watts (ed.): *Science in the National Curriculum*

J. Wilson: *A New Introduction to Moral Education*

S. Wolfendale *et al.* (eds): *The Profession and Practice of Educational Psychology: Future Directions*

Religious Education in the Primary School

Managing Diversity

Elizabeth Hughes

CASSELL

Cassell

Villiers House
41/47 Strand
London WC2N 5JE

387 Park Avenue South
New York
NY 10016–8810

First published 1994

British Library Cataloguing-in-Publication Data
A catalogue record for this book is available from the British Library.

ISBN 0-304-32658-5 (hardback)
       0-304-32656-9 (paperback)

Acknowledgements

The author and publisher wish to thank the following for permission to reprint copyright material. Although every effort has been made to contact the owners of the copyright material reproduced in this book, it has not been possible to trace all of them. If such owners contact the publisher, the appropriate acknowledgements will appear in any future editions.

Anon, 'Dialectic of Prayer and Praxis', quoted in J. Cullinan, *The Month* (May 1981). Reprinted by permission of the publisher.

Margaret Atwood, 'The Sin Eater', from *Dancing Girls and Other Stories*, published by Jonathan Cape. Reprinted by permission of the publisher.

Edward Bond, 'Sonnet 10' and 'Deciding', from *Poems 1978–1985*, published by Methuen London. Reprinted by permission of the publisher.

Bertold Brecht, 'Deliver the Goods', from *Poems 1913–1956*, translated by Humphrey Milnes, published by Methuen London. Reprinted by permission of the publisher.

Ruth Fainlight, 'The Other', from *The Bloodaxe Book of Contemporary Women Poets*, ed. Jeni Couzyn, published by Bloodaxe Books Limited. Reprinted by permission of the publisher.

Robert Frost, 'Mending a Wall', from *The Complete Poems of Robert Frost*, ed. Edward Connery Lathem, published by Jonathan Cape Limited. Reprinted by permission of the publisher and the Estate of Robert Frost.

Robert Graves, 'In Broken Images' from *Collected Poems 1975* and 'The Thieves' from *Collected Poems 1965*. Reprinted by permission of A.P. Watt Limited on behalf of The Trustees of the Robert Graves Copyright Trust.

C.H. Sisson, 'Sonnet', from *Antidotes*, published by Carcanet Press Limited. Reprinted by permission of the publisher.

Stevie Smith, 'The Frog Prince' from *The Frog Prince and Other Poems*. Reprinted by permission of James MacGibbon, as executor of the Estate of Stevie Smith.

Dylan Thomas, 'Ears in the turret hear', from *The Poems*, published by J.M. Dent. Reprinted by permission of David Higham Associates Limited.

Typeset by Colset Private Limited, Singapore
Printed and bound in Great Britain by Redwood Books, Trowbridge, Wilts.

Contents

Preface

When one embarks on a long-term piece of school-based research, there is a persistent worry that the projected book will be irrelevant to the educational agenda at the time of publication.

Reassuringly, this book is a timely contribution to the on-going debate about the purpose and content of RE in the school curriculum. It explores the factors which influence staff work on RE policy and practice and is a resource for those who are undertaking such work in response to the 1993 Education Act or impending inspection. This book reflects on school events and situations in the late 1980s, offering working principles and management strategies for RE policy-making appropriate for the 1990s. It identifies *difference* as the vital educational issue which influences staff relations and curriculum content.

In 1986, when the research work was in its design stage, I searched to find a suitable name for the enterprise. The focus was the Religious Education curriculum; its emphasis on whole-staff participation gave it a Teacher Education thrust; and the use of group relations theory and working methods carried a Management dimension. Playing with the letters MTECRE, I made the startling discovery that I was in danger of running CREMATE (Curriculum, RE, Management and Teacher Education). Religious Education was a hot potato and the work would involve flare-ups and fire-fighting. But the acronym hardly represented the original constructive vision of enhanced RE provision and increased teacher competence which inspired the project. So Management was dropped from the title, leaving the initiative with the more optimistic designation CREATE (Curriculum RE and Teacher Education).

The Education Acts of 1988 and 1993 provide conditions for the results of this work to be taken up and thrive. There are many situations which could be informed by the insights and approaches of this book: preparation for RE inspections, staff and governor co-operation in policy-making, and using the subject co-ordinator as an internal consultant.

The Framework for Inspection allows for examination of the standards achieved by pupils, commentary upon the efficacy of school management and a structured search for evidence of whole-school curriculum policies as the bedrock of classroom and staffroom life. This will propel schools towards INSET which develops teachers' capacity to take a role in group work. The classroom teacher of the future will need the ability to engage in adult professional dialogue about the management of learning. Increasingly, directed time will be spent in policy meetings, to discern or review current theory and practice.

Schools will need INSET provision to facilitate co-operative working styles, as the rush to manufacture staff-and governor-supported cross-curricular policies on such sensitive issues as worship, moral and spiritual development, discipline, education for personal relationships and sex education, special needs, citizenship and staff development.

This type of work will be new to many who have filled filing cabinets with school mission statements, development plans and curricular policies written in private by a committee of one. Inspection will be swift to identify policies whose only effect on school life has been to occupy space in a box-file.

Initial teacher training had no brief for ensuring that students had management skills beyond the level needed to implement the policies of others and organize children's learning. Management and group skills courses have traditionally been the preserve of the aspirant headteacher, master's degree candidate or those in a secondary school who hold a pastoral responsibility. If autocratic and authoritarian leadership styles are giving way to a more consensual exercise of influence, expertise and responsibility, generic group relations skills will be an advantage for all.

Trained and untrained alike, groups in every school in the land will have to manage their being together. They will do this with different degrees of success and address their tasks variously paralysed by unconscious anxieties or sensitive to the different fears, values and life stances they represent. Therefore, training is not an optional extra, it is a life-line for groups about to enter the cross-curricular Bermuda Triangle.

Consultancy-based RE development work could be the 'double whammy' of the INSET world, providing generic skills training together with support for work on a difficult curriculum area which looks set to receive significant attention in the first round of inspections.

RE inspection will apply to all schools. In the county maintained sector, it will be carried out by the Registered Inspector's team. In the voluntary aided sector, the bishop is required by Section 13 of the 1993 Act to appoint diocesan inspectors to carry out an inspection of denominational RE. This legislation has surprised some who saw the setting up of SACREs in 1988 as a government withdrawal from RE involvement. This attitude ignores the fact that the National Curriculum consists of the core curriculum *plus* RE and worship. It also ignores the frantic political debate about the legality of many syllabuses, produced and authorized by SACREs, whose content is not clearly weighted towards Christianity. RE is back on the political agenda with pundits from the right-wing Policy Unit arguing that Christianity is the key to preserving national norms of culture identity and moral behaviour. Not since the conversion of Constantine has there been such support for religion as the glue to hold the nation together. John Patten, two weeks before he became Secretary of State for Education, published his view that promotion of the fear of God in schools and a greater sense of guilt would reduce the crime rate. The political furore about religion and education seems set to run for a while.

Meanwhile members of SACREs wonder what will happen to them and their statutory obligations, if LEAs, their sponsoring bodies, disappear, as Mr Patten has forecast.

Recent research has shown that the proportion of time given to RE has dropped since the introduction of the National Curriculum and Key Stage testing. In some schools it was swallowed up into 'topic work' or cross-curricular themes in an uncritical way. Thus it was effectively denied to pupils and dropped from staff concern.

The return of RE on a tide of political zeal will make some reach for their INSET budgets, looking for external support for policy and curriculum work. Consultancy-based approaches may be vital to staff groups, who, like the present government, find that they have to dig up the RE bomb that was buried in 1988.

Mention of unexploded bombs recalls my own moments of reluctant enthusiasm for the work of CREATE. I was not always confident that in five years one could discover what lay behind primary teachers' difficulties with RE in a pluralist society and come up with suggestions for a way forward. At times, I felt like the man ordered by the king to teach his favourite monkey to talk within five years. His wife found his sanguine attitude difficult to understand. But he explained, 'In five years the king could die, the monkey could die, I could die – or I might just teach the monkey to talk.'

I am grateful to those people whose encouragement saw me through moments when the task looked impossible – Paul and Mary Morris, Lorna Crossman, Margaret Crompton and Marian Lucas. Thanks are due to the following people and organizations, who offered advice, enthusiasm and critical support: Sheila Hunter, Dr Anne Edwards, The Grubb Institute, Dr Brian Gates and the CREATE Steering Committee, and Sandra Margolies at Cassell. Thanks are especially due to the All Saints Trust, which funded CREATE, St Martin's College, Lancaster, which hosted it, and Maria Chippendale, who cheerfully typed the manuscript.

Part One

Traditional Sensitivities

The opening chapter of this book describes the personal and professional conflicts that primary teachers face in addressing differences of religious, religious educational and moral values in the school curriculum. In Chapter 2 it is argued that recent National Curriculum Council encouragement to debate the core values of education will be difficult to realize within the educational culture and philosophy generated by the Education Reform Act 1988 and the National Curriculum. The ways that differences are domesticated and dissolved in the primary school context are described in Chapter 3.

Chapter 1

All Change

I come from the town of Mira,
Beyond the Bridges of St Clare
I don't suppose you've heard of Mira,
It's very small, but it's there,
They have the very greenest trees,
And skies as bright as flame
But what I liked the most about Mira
Was just everybody knew my name.

A street that is strange is never cosy,
A room that is strange is never sweet,
I wish to find a chair that knows me,
And walk a street that knows my feet.
I'm very far from Mira now,
And there's no turning back.
I've got to find a place, I need to find a place,
Where everything is still the same.

A street where I can go,
With people that I know.
Where everybody knows my name.
Can you imagine that,
Can you imagine that
Everybody knew my name.

'Mira' (Irish folk song)

'Nobody told us it was going to be like this. The world has changed so much. We aren't prepared for it. At college, 25 years ago the lecturers described the kind of schools we'd be likely to teach in. They don't exist anymore. They could never have even imagined a school like this with such a high Muslim intake. No wonder we are floundering with RE.'

(Fieldnote, St Benedict's RC)

A sense of discomfort with change inspires the words of this primary school teacher. Her words were spoken with strong feeling generated by daily struggles to work creatively with the conflicting demands of teaching in a Roman Catholic school which has 70 per cent ethnic minority pupils.

The teacher's comment recognizes the changing social environment and her perceived inability to respond to it. She also acknowledges that her sense of being stuck, casting about like a fish out of water, is shared by her colleagues. They are united in that they have been overtaken by social, racial and religious developments in society without adequate knowledge, understanding or skills to cope.

This is an experience common to all people in late twentieth-century Britain. However, the teacher feels required to respond differently from a bus conductor, doctor or business manager. The educators' task of initiating pupils into cultural tradition is both highlighted and made more difficult by long-term social development and renegotiation. Teachers feel guilty about their inability to manufacture and transmit 'instant tradition' to pupils even as social change is taking place. Society expects the educational agenda to include inducting pupils into the prevailing culture by handing on received tradition. This is a difficult requirement to meet when cultural norms and values are being challenged and revised and there is a general lack of consensus. This lies behind teachers' feeling of falling short in the representative and inductive dimensions of their work, even though there is no national agreement on what should be represented as British values, norms and identity. The insistence that children should be offered a stable and predictable culture may be one way that the wider population denies the extensive social and religious change currently taking place.

FEAR OF CHANGE

People fear and resist changes, whether they affect domestic routines or the RE programmes offered in schools. Our notion of 'a nice change' is restricted to holidays or pleasant social encounters. Most of the time those we like are encouraged to take care because 'we don't want anything to happen'. This 'happening' is always imagined as an unwarranted change for the worse. Feeling secure with a present which is at least known and reliable, we resist change in case the new situation proves unmanageable. This is especially true in the case of changes that affect work, where inadequate response to a new dynamic can lead to feelings of incompetence and low self-esteem. This is felt particularly in teaching where personal identity is often tied in with a sense of professional vocation.

There are three standard responses to dealing with change. In the first instance one can refuse to recognize that any new stimulus exists in the environment. A second response is to limit change by tinkering with some structures or working methods, modifying rather than rethinking established practice. The third response is to view change as a process and recognize that the task of the able respondent is to work fluidly with traditions, newly emergent values and issues to create new cultural understandings adequate for the future.

Educators are challenged to shape their policies, institutions and pedagogy according to the last response. Modes one and two may provide a temporary defence against development but are inadequate to the reality of societal evolution.

It is tempting to handle upheaval or stress by the method of rational organization. It is comforting to believe that there is a logical administrative approach which would make for a pain-free change process. But change is not something pliantly subject to control or edit. It is experienced as overwhelming people and institutions, trailing emotional turbulence in its wake.

> I built my house by the sea.
> Not on the sands, mind you;
> not on the shifting sand.
> And I built it of rock.
> A strong house
> by a strong sea.
> And we got well acquainted, the sea and I.
> Good neighbours.
> Not that we spoke much.
> We met in silences.
> Respectful, keeping our distance,
> but looking our thought across the fence of sand.
> Always, the fence of sand our barrier,
> always, the sand between.
>
> And then one day,
> – and I still don't know how it happened –
> the sea came.
> Without warning.
> Without welcome, even.
> Not sudden and swift, but a shifting across the sand like wine.
> Less like the flow of water than the flow of blood.
> Slow, but coming.
> Slow, but flowing like an open wound.
> And I thought of flight and I thought of drowning and I thought of death.
> And while I thought the sea crept higher, till it reached my door.
> And I knew, then, there was neither flight, nor death, nor drowning,
> That when the sea comes calling you stop being good neighbours
> Well acquainted, friendly-at-a-distance, neighbours
> And you give your house for a coral castle,
> And you learn to breathe underwater.[1]

Our sympathy and passions are actively engaged by the situation described in the poem. The relentless advance of change cannot be reversed by the administrative commands of a latter-day Canute. Survival is possible only by painful adaptation, equivalent to the painful exchange of nose and lung for gills. It requires the sacrifice of the known environment and historic securities for a more fluid context.

However, human history, and religious history in particular, shows that people have a preference for fixed categories and absolute statements. The way we used to be is the way we want to continue. Everyone prefers that certainties and norms learned and established in early life should continue to the third and fourth generation. In sponsoring this the appearance of the new is denied.

Nasruddin became prime minister to the king. Once, while he wandered through the palace, he saw a royal falcon.

Now Nasruddin had never seen this kind of a pigeon before. So he got out a pair of scissors and trimmed the claws, the wings, and the beak of the falcon. 'Now you look like a decent bird,' he said. 'Your keeper had evidently been neglecting you.'[2]

Whilst Nasruddin's is a common response, it provides no model for the transformations being sought in British self-understanding at this time. Living out old stories encourages us to enact old behaviours that are inadequate to the present situation. The key task for educators is to discover how to use tradition and history as a resource to build the future. This requires working with the totality of available experience so that empowering stories can be created for those who will live in a new world.

> My grandfather·was paralysed. Once he was asked to tell a story about his teacher and he told how the Holy Baal Shem Tov used to jump and dance when he was praying. My grandfather stood up while he was telling the story and the story carried him away so much that he had to jump and dance to show how the master had done it. From that moment, he was healed. This is how stories ought to be told.[3]

The engagement which transforms is active and participatory. This short narrative challenges its hearers to embody it in their quest for social change. As the grandfather in the story harnesses the full power of his experience of prayer, existing resources from history, tradition and commitment can empower others to take new social steps. The task of enacting change will be paralysed if it deteriorates into repetition of tired axioms about the nature of change.

The real work is to tell a new social story which sponsors public institutions and attitudes that will help pupils to become citizens comfortable with pluralism. Primary school practice gives RE a key role in relation to pluralism. In many schools multifaith RE carries the entire multicultural dimension of the curriculum. This gives the impression that teachers see issues of culture, race and pluralism as directly dependent upon world faith systems. Since this is patently not the case, the prevalence of this practice leads to the suspicion that RE and RE topic work are being used to process problematic issues that have not been thought through.

If RE is to make a useful contribution to the educational and social development of pupils

1. staff need a clear rationale for the RE curriculum they offer;
2. staff need to consider the implications of work on pluralism and difference for the whole curriculum culture and ethos of the school.

DIFFERENCE AND THE EDUCATIONAL DEBATE

It appears that people in our society see cultural pluralism as a threat rather than an opportunity. Genuine pluralism is disturbing and costly. Foreign perspectives on the world put us in touch with unflattering interpretations of national heroes. They question the justice of historical practices which built an empire. Old loyalties and self-understanding can be disrupted when one hears history from the mouths of people who represent themselves as oppressed by it. There is no cultural bastion that is secure from such a critique.

Themes relating to societal norms and differences have recurred in educational documents, policy and debate over the past ten years. But their relation to each other and precisely which themes are dominant remains unclear. The school curriculum can work as a reference for a given society's image of itself and its values. But the curriculum which we have in 1993 is difficult to construe as a whole vision. It can only be viewed as fragments. Perhaps that does give an image of Britain at the beginning of the 1990s, fragmented in search of a set of values and a sense of wholeness.

In schools, teachers variously praise and question aspects of recent reforms. They offer different views of curriculum changes and give conflicting explanations of the 'new values' in education. In 1986 L. Beyer argued

> What is needed is a way of making sense of current educational institutions, a comprehensive view of education that is both incisive as theory and helpful as practice. Perhaps more importantly such an understanding might procure the sort of changes that go beyond mere reform to social and educational transformation.[4]

The Education Reform Act of 1988 did not meet any of his basic requirements let alone supply a transforming vision of Britishness. The nationality distress became clear in April 1990, around the time when British and French Channel Tunnel drilling teams met up and shook hands in what was now a corridor linking Britain and France. At the very moment that the frontiers of the sceptred isle were sundered Norman Tebbit sought to offer boundaries for Britishness by suggesting that Asians living in Britain should support the national cricket team. The synchronicity of the two events threw into focus the quest for 'nationality security' in the face of encroachment by 'foreigners'. Just what did it mean to be British? Politicians appeared to operate with an understanding which was implicitly conformist.

If such understanding remains implicit it is difficult to examine its adequacy or the policy decisions which follow from it. The government's lack of regard for theoretical debate offers a superficial attraction. It curtails political controversy by shrouding the issue in fog. But it is important now to shed the idea that a fixed and historical idea of British identity or culture is either possible or desirable. All identities and cultures are historically located. They change over time or the culture dies.

History can hold the present in a paralysing grip. Hindsight provides a clear perspective and grants wholeness of vision to the educational philosophies and methods which gave coherence to the educational practice of an earlier era. In Britain this has been idealized to the extent that people talk as if there was a mythic Golden Age when all Britons lived united by a common culture and shared belief. By hook or by crook or by Education Act the nation is trying to return to Never Never Land.

Strong passions are a feature of curriculum work.

> The curriculum, it is not melodramatic to declare, is the battleground for an intellectual civil war and the battle for cultural authority is a wayward often intermittently fierce, always protracted, and always fervent one. Its different guerillas include parents, pupils, teachers, bureaucrats, left, right, centre, nationalities and the compelling mercenaries of the market forces.[5]

While educationalists disagree and politicians row and fudge issues, teachers are left delivering the sum of the parts of the National Curriculum, confused about what vision of nationhood they are being asked to hand on.

THE PRIMARY SCHOOL AND THE POLITICS OF CHANGE

The telling of new social stories is the job of the politician, who beguiles the electorate with visions of a future utopia. The promise always takes the same form: dreams achieving substance tomorrow by the application of ideology today. The policies of opponents are presented in a caricatured form guaranteed to evoke derision.

Current educational debate is marked by similar posturing and slogans designed to secure institutional or curriculum control. Arguments over the purpose of primary education can be battles between stereotyped positions. Campaigners for child centredness suggest

> The purpose of primary education is to foster the development of the child's individuality and independence enabling him to discover his own talents and interests, find a full enjoyment of life in his own way and acquire his own attitudes towards society.[6]

Those who emphasize the societal purpose of education counter with

> The purpose of primary education is to begin to equip the child with skills and attitudes which will enable him to take his place effectively and competently in society, fitting him to make a choice of an occupational role and to live harmoniously in his community.[7]

When these alternatives are offered as mutually exclusive conflict is inevitable. This polarization of the needs of the child and society have been a feature of primary education debates since Plowden.

Education is always a political activity. The dominant themes in education arise from particular historical settings and are connected to the values and social and political aims of a given society. Curriculum decisions about how to teach reading or the content of the history syllabus reflect political influence. The status and relations between teachers and pupils which apply in a class-room also mirror authority structures in the wider society. In balancing the freedoms of the individual with the requirements of the larger group the teacher is engaged in the act of government writ small.

In 1982 White suggested that

> of all members of the teaching profession [the primary teacher] has traditionally been the least politically aware. Her typical milieu has been the world of arts and crafts, of movement and drama, of learning to read and count. It has typically been a cosy world looking inward quietly, cut off from the complexities of politics.[8]

Professional insularity is not useful for those who are increasingly required to help children make sense of an ambiguous world. The teacher may well be described as one who midwives the future from pupils' present. But others have a large investment in that future which will be influenced by teacher values, expectations and norms. It is not surprising that the public and politicians place teachers under great scrutiny because the meanings, interpretations and possibilities which will affect the future are created in the class-room.

CONFLICT, CONVICTION AND CONFUSION

Worry about social change prompts the public to peer over the shoulders of the teachers appointed to act on behalf of all. Each pair of eyes possesses a unique perspective on life constructed out of personal allegiances to groups and values, beliefs about humanity and God, preferences about educational practices and formative memories of their own school days. The outsider looking in carries the baggage of damaging uncritical assumptions, informed concern, and goodwill. In this, the observer resembles the teacher. How could it be otherwise? Teacher, parent, governor, Minister of State or inspector – all are shaped by their commitments and partialities. The educational arena can provide an opportunity for people to act out of these loyalties on behalf of the next generation. But expressed concern about the schooling of the nation's children can also lead to rows about the preordinate value of some or another loyalty such as individualism, traditional family values, religious commitment, economic awareness or vocationalism.

British society enjoys a reputation for civilization. There is a well-developed code of social behaviour designed to maintain good relations by excising controversy from social gatherings. This code reaches its apogee in the rules governing talk at a regimental dinner. As this rather boozy event will be attended by men wearing swords, topics recognized as stirring the passions – sex, religion and politics – are striken from the menu of permitted discourse. Thus the war-time warning 'careless talk costs lives' comes into its own!

No such veto appears on the agenda topics for staff, governors' or parents' meetings in the primary school. There policies on sex education, worship and religious education, and education for citizenship are tussled over in an atmosphere of passionate sobriety. It is tempting to see the primary curriculum as the designated battle zone for a national fight about British convictions and values.

DIFFERENCE ON THE AGENDA

This puts difference at the centre of the educational agenda in a number of ways. Teachers as a group do not have a common pool of values or shared philosophy. The convictions they represent in their professional practice are properly their own by virtue of personal development rather than professional training. Great disagreement over a religious education programme is just as likely at a staff meeting in a voluntary aided school as at one held in the county maintained school down the road. In both situations the professional opportunity to voice strongly felt disagreement about religion and morals within a cohesive group raises fears that ideological rifts will tear that group apart.

Talk of difference tends to treat 'it' as a thing and a problematic thing. The tone tends to be conciliatory, concerned with dissolving or resolving difference, replacing 'it' with consensus. Difference is not a thing, but a useful way of naming the positions of two or more persons or groups *vis-à-vis* a situation, policy or belief. Difference describes relationships between people rather than identifying objects or situations.

Turning the spotlight on difference forces recognition of the place of emotion and strong feeling in the day-to-day life of the staffroom. Some would see this as dangerous because it challenges the widespread notion that logic and reason can solve any problem. This belief is an essential part of the educational enterprise. There are well-developed academic methods and forms for the critique of ideas and theories but there is no comparable tradition in education for critical engagement with commitment and feelings. The general impression is that feelings cloud the judgement and that prospects for intellectual improvement are better without them. Thus the educational process tends to divorce reason and emotion, doing violence to the way in which people experience the totality of their lives.

Deep personal feeling is a notable feature of human experience. But teachers fight shy of it in an educational practice which encourages pupils to reach value decisions on the basis of value-free information. The connections between values, feelings, commitments, loyalties and identity remain largely unexplored except in relation to generalizations about the roots of prejudice and bias. Emotion and the expression of strong feelings are systematically negated. Elliot Eisner talks about school having a 'null curriculum'[9], that which is not taught. This includes ways of being and doing tacitly regarded as inappropriate for handling and understanding life. Dealing with difference is part of the British null curriculum. Afraid that a disagreement may occur, there is a tendency to avoid the struggle with lived differences in class-room and staffroom discussion. Eric Fromm feared that 'The child starts with giving up the expression of his feeling and eventually gives up the very feeling itself'[10]. The roots of this repression can be traced to a persistent strand in educational thinking.

> The cool distanced tone of the philosopher has come down through the centuries, yet in its very detachment it has displayed the disquiet felt before the unruly and threatening nature of human emotions. The discomposure is evidenced as philosphers address themselves to the education of the emotions, seeking to domesticate them and subject them to the order and control of reason.[11]

The affectional capacities which have been voted off the educational agenda exert great influence on the politics of human beings. Lives are made up of

> characteristic elements of impulse, restraint and tone; specifically affective elements of unconsciousness and relationships; not feeling against thought, but thought as felt and feeling as thought: practical consciousness of a kind present in a living and interrelated continuity.[12]

If there is an unwritten rule that all of this is to be ignored or repressed, educationalists can hardly claim to have tamed the emotional beast, but merely to have driven it into the underground of the unconscious. One is reminded of John Cleese in *Fawlty Towers* trying to wrestle with anti-German feelings. 'Whatever you do, don't mention the war' was to be the watchword for hotel staff in the presence of their European visitors. But the short stay was continually punctuated by Freudian slips and unconscious references to World War II. Being off the official agenda, repressed feelings and events can control the whole agenda.

If difference is to be taken seriously by teachers and others engaged in the educational dialogue they must develop connections to

1. the variety of the wider social world;
2. the unconscious internal concerns of staff and pupils.

MAKING A WORLD OF DIFFERENCE

People constantly break and remake the small 'worlds' in which they live. When they speak of the 'worlds' of RE, science, art, the child, the school and the family they are highlighting the worth of each of these as a focus for experience. It also exemplifies the human tendency to break up life into manageable pieces. To the mother, the family is all, and to the teacher, the school. These constitute the fixed points from which all events, public policies and values are monitored. These 'worlds' are ideas in the mind, more or less accurate mental pictures developed to guide and organize personal and professional action. A constant factor in all work is the maintenance of these 'worlds', which are only modified when they begin to do real damage.

For example, it may not be useful to see the primary school world in terms of 'safe haven' or 'one big happy family'. Despite the desire to see a school as a secure and autonomous unit, it cannot thrive if staff and pupils behave as if it is a separate domain isolated from events and attitudes in a diverse society. There needs to be a dialogue about *interdependence*. However much a school staff declares that the school badge should be a smiley face, the staff and pupils cannot thrive under an imposed unitary culture and identity. Behind the crest, the family members can be at each other's throats, unable to tolerate the differences among themselves. There needs to be a dialogue about the degree of *independence* essential to maintain a lively, though coherent, organization.

This book explores the complex task of managing primary school RE in a time of educational and social change. The focus is on the staff dynamics of curriculum development. It presents recent school-based research which highlights anxiety about diversity as a factor which inhibits curriculum renewal. It recommends Group Relations theory and working methods as a resource for the analysis and interpretation of the staffroom conflicts which hinder curriculum development in RE.

It is a book for teachers interested in widening their perceptions so that they can increase professional options. Developing wider perspectives encourages people to see their own situation in a new way. The first step in changing your 'world' is to change your mind.

NOTES AND REFERENCES

1. Anonymous, quoted in J. Cullinan, 'Dialectic of prayer and praxis', *The Month* (May 1981), 165–71.
2. A. de Mello (1984) *Song of the Bird* (New York: Image Books, Doubleday), p. 7.
3. Hassidic tale attributed to Martin Buber, quoted in N. Perrin (1967) *Rediscovering the Teaching of Jesus* (New York: Harper & Row), p. 118.
4. L. Beyer, L. 'The parameters of educational enquiry', *Curriculum Enquiry II* (January–March 1986), 87–105.
5. F. Inglis (1985) *The Management of Ignorance* (London: Blackwell), p. 23.
6. P. M. E. Ashton, P. Keen, F. Davies and B. J. Holley (1975) *The Aims of Primary Education: A Study of Teachers' Opinions* (London: Macmillan), p. 38.
7. *Ibid.*
8. J. White (1982) 'The primary teacher as servant of the State', in C. Richards (ed.), *New Directions in Primary Education* (Brighton: Falmer Press), p. 203.
9. E. Eisner (1979) *The Educational Imagination* (New York: Macmillan), pp. 83–92.
10. E. Fromm (1942) *The Fear of Freedom* (London: Routledge & Kegan Paul), pp. 209–10.
11. R. Gibson (1986) *Critical Theory and Education* (London: Hodder & Stoughton), pp. 118–19.
12. R. Williams (1977) *Marxism and Literature* (Oxford: OUP), p. 132.

Chapter 2

RE and the Staff Group 1988–93

I stepped from Plank to Plank
A slow and cautious way
The Stars about my Head I felt
About my Feet the Sea.

I knew not but the next
Would be my final inch –
This gave me that precarious Gait
Some call Experience.

Emily Dickinson, 'I Stepped from Plank to Plank'[1]

Progress towards the future appears to depend on the crossing of a rickety bridge pieced together from worn-out practices and green, untested ideas. The mature tread warily, knowing that the way will be perilous, beset by change and unexpected turnabouts. There will be relief in finding an old timber which holds, a new plank which has not warped in the weather. Given the trying nature of negotiating history, it is understandable that we try to offer the next generation a blueprint so that difference does not appear overwhelming.

DIFFERENCE AND CONSENSUS IN PRIMARY SCHOOL CULTURE

The exploration of differences is essential to learning in the primary setting. Teachers in primary schools display ambiguous attitudes towards difference. On the one hand variety of religion, culture, customs and costume provides a useful source of stimulus material. These kinds of differences are a never ending source of attention. By contrast, difference, in the sense of disagreement or conflict, tends to be labelled as the outcome of bad or undesirable behaviour. Pupils are not encouraged to value this, and curriculum opportunities for learning about conflict, and even more so learning from it, are difficult to find in the primary school.

Schools encourage pupils to differentiate. When the pupil can distinguish between alphabetical or numerical symbols, literacy and numeracy are possible. Without a capacity to distinguish between black and white it would be impossible to read a page of text. The underlying dynamic of many early lessons is 'not this, but that'. The ability to divide up and categorize the world is basic to understanding it.

With this capacity to discriminate comes the inclination to evaluate. Schools teach pupils to judge and identify elements of experience as more or less valuable, important or significant. Pupils are taught a vocabulary for this prioritization: good, better, best. The child who demonstrates a talent for critical discrimination and produces finely honed distinctions is said to be clever.

However, the capacity to differentiate is a two-edged sword. The tendency to jump from discrimination to prejudice is there in both language and experience. Discrimination interpreted this way is threatening to good human relationships. Education in the primary years places great importance on teaching children to get on with others and a variety of strategies are employed to this end. They involve the setting of rules covering permissible and non-permissible activity in large group settings. Teacher advice and penalties reinforce these norms so that the child is introduced to and conformed by the social consensus mediated through the curriculum. Education has a multiplicity of aims but it works on behalf of society as a whole to initiate children into a productive and tolerably harmonious adult community.

The school itself is a melting pot for the cultures and value variety brought in by the pupils. One testimony to the success of school as an apprenticeship for social life may be that in the face of this variety pupils adopt shared fashions, pop idols and cultural icons which are displayed on T-shirts and badges and offered for sale as toys. Most pupils certainly adopt and live in a consensual peer culture as a preface to adulthood. But this does not necessarily indicate mastery of the skills of harmonious living. Much publicity has been given to those children excluded by their peers because they do not have the 'right' brand of footwear or the latest fashion item. The Elton Report's high-lighting of bullying in schools and the Burnage Report's exploration of racism in one school suggest a current of violence in some schools based on discrimination and the development of cliques.

Teachers find themselves with the ambiguous task of fostering and valuing differentiation whilst challenging its unjust application in social relations. This is a tall order. Attempts to address this disconcerting ambiguity through explicit curricular programmes will only be successful if the teachers working with them are aware of the complex interests, histories and perceptions involved.

RELIGION, RE AND GROUPS

One way of handling ambiguity is to posit a superordinate institution which draws conflicting strands into a seamless unity. Durkheim recognized that society gave this role to religion, which he described as 'the symbolic representation of integration'. Since religion is seen to provide identity and cohesiveness to groups and has been a unifying force in the life of nations in the past, it is not surprising that schools appropriate it to build a sense of community. However, the type of community born out of corporate religious beliefs and expressions can not be constituted from the loose collectivity of pupils and teachers in a maintained school being obliged to use the ritual trappings of hymns and prayers. Community based on religious commitment is antithetical to liberal attempts at camaraderie. Buber pointed out:

> Community is where community happens. Collectivity is based on an organized atrophy of personal existence, community on its increase and confirmation in life lived towards one another. The modern zeal for collectivity is a flight from community's testing and consecration of the person, a flight from the vital dialogue, demanding the staking of the self, which is the heart of the world.[2]

In saying this he emphasizes the passionate commitment required by religious community over against the *laissez-faire* relations of secular institutions.

Though it is appealing to see religions as united by a common content of faith based on peace on earth and goodwill to all people this is a simplistic misrepresentation. The commonality of faith traditions lies in the hopes of transcendence they hold out in situations of anguish and limitation, and their reticence in offering the kingdom of God, Nirvana or paradise on a plate. Furthermore, each religion has its own narratives and understanding of how transcendence comes about, expressed in doctrines which often claim scandalously exclusive access to divine power.

Religion in the 1990s is more notable for its inter-faith feuding than the efficacy of dialogue. Calls for a Holy War, battles to tear down the Amritsar temple and erect a Hindu shrine, clashes between Christian and Muslim militia in the former Yugoslavia are typical evening news items. In the face of this international experience, religious issues and RE in schools have become a source of conflict in current educational discourse.

Religious strife and fighting between interest groups has been a particular aspect of the educational debate in the 1980s. The parliamentary discussion of the Education Reform Act 1988 revealed strong feeling for and against Religious Education as a curriculum component and worship as a compulsory part of the school day. It was felt politically unwise to legislate for RE at government level and though RE was declared to be an essential part of the National Curriculum, it was not included in the core curriculum, which was to be subject to the guidance of the National Curriculum Council. RE was given over to the care of SACREs (Standing Advisory Councils for Religious Education), bodies of religiously diverse people recruited by LEAs to design an Agreed Syllabus judged appropriate for maintained schools in that locality. These groups were to oversee RE to ensure that provision within a given education authority complied with the law. This decision to delegate solved Parliament's problem and moved dispute and debate about RE into the regions in the late 1980s.

In the 1990s, as schools opt out and the future of LEAs looks insecure, there is growing uncertainty about the maintenance of these RE monitoring provisions. This has led some people to wonder if RE will be given adequate curriculum time in the future. Some of the authors of the Swann Report may take heart at this. Although they wrote of RE as contributing to anti-racism, the report had a suspicion of the whole RE endeavour. It eventually advocated multifaith RE teaching as an anti-racist and public order strategy.

> Unless major efforts are made to reconcile the concerns and aspirations of both the majority and minority communities along more genuinely pluralist lines, there is a real risk of the fragmentation of our society along ethnic lines which would seriously threaten the stability and cohesion of society as a whole . . .[3]

Much of the task in countering and overcoming racism is concerned with attitude change and encouraging youngsters to develop positive attitudes towards the multiracial nature of society, free from the influence of inaccurate myths and stereotypes and other ethnic groups.[4]

When the report refers directly to religion, however, it is preoccupied with its perceived deleterious secular and social implications. It went on to advocate phenomenological approaches to RE 'as the only response that accords with the fundamental principles underlying the ideal of cultural pluralism.'[5] This does phenomenological RE no favours since the principles Swann puts forward offer secular, social and cultural ideologies as the arbiters of good practice. Swann rejected confessional RE aims or strategies for religious formation of pupils as inappropriate for a multibelief society.

At the same time there was pressure from Muslim groups for voluntary aided status for some Islamic schools. All but six members of the Swann committee were opposed to the extension of separate provision and acknowledged that

our conclusion about the desirability of denominational voluntary aided schools for Muslims, or other groups by extension, seriously calls into question the long established dual system of educational provision in this country and particularly the role of the churches in the provision of education.[6]

This restatement of opposition to voluntary aided schools called to mind earlier secularist calls for their abolition on the grounds that they offered evangelism on the rates. In the 1980s commentators described Britain as a post-Christian culture. A.D. Gilbert fills out this statement:

A post-Christian society is not one from which Christianity has departed, but one in which it has become marginal. It is a society where to be unreligious is to be normal, where to think and act in secular terms is to be conventional, where neither status nor responsibility depends on religious faith. Some members of such a society continue to find Christianity a profound, vital influence on their lives, but in so doing they place themselves outside the mainstream of social life and culture.[7]

Pupils and teachers in the nation's primary school system are drawn from this society. Secularism and the consequences of secularity therefore have significant impact on teachers' RE planning and teaching.

THE PRIMARY STAFF GROUP 1988–93

The differences, disagreements and ideologies prevalent in society as a whole are reflected in the thoughts and actions of staff in school. Government attention to religion and education encouraged staffroom conversation on the curriculum role and function of RE for the few days that the media gave it coverage. Teacher interest in the late 1980s and early 1990s was centred on the style and structure of core curriculum subjects and the practical implications of planning for Attainment Targets (ATs), Standard Assessment Tasks (SATs) and Key Stage testing.

The National Curriculum came about because the educational system was seen as so inefficient as to put the nation's economic and technological progress at risk. The Education Reform Act of 1988 began the efficiency drive. Since then the work of teachers has become increasingly bureaucratic because of national educational planning to promote 'a return to basics', 'higher standards', 'efficiency and accountability', and the 'extension of the curriculum'.

Control over content, teaching and evaluation moved outside the school. The first stage of this process was the separation of curriculum and syllabus conception from its execution. Imposed programmes of study, broken down into Attainment Targets and Assessment Tests, meant that teachers began to lose sight of and control of the unity of their work. People external to the situation in school were the curriculum designers, monitors and evaluators. The teachers 'deliver' the programme. This threatens to lead to the de-skilling of teachers.

> When individuals cease to plan and control a large portion of their own work, the skills essential to doing these tasks self-reflectively and well atrophy and are forgotten. The skills that teachers have built up over decades of hard work – setting relevant curricular goals, establishing content, designing lessons and instructional strategies . . . are lost. In many ways, given the centralisation of authority and control, they are simply no longer needed. In the process, however, the very things that make teaching a professional activity – the control of one's own expertise and time – are also dissipated.[8]

Teaching and factory work were beginning to have a lot in common.

> It is convenient for governments, local authorities and parents to see it [school] as a factory. Then they can ask it to deliver particular types of goods, they can use the language of resource and output, they can improve quality control and other regulations, they can measure and compare effectiveness.[9]

Teachers began to complain of 'alienation' and 'burn-out'. These phenomena are often described as individual psychological responses to stress. This description masks the structural origin of the problem created by teachers' lack of control over their day-to-day work.

The extension of the primary curriculum to include ten subjects (in which the primary teachers themselves have to be proficient to at least Key Stage 4 level) has exacerbated the difficulties. The burden is further increased by the intensification of the workload in terms of paper work for assessment monitoring and regulatory purposes. The aim of work well done is being replaced with relief at work completed, as time becomes a rare commodity. Dependence on external experts and packaged programmes which offer a map through the educational quicksands is increasing.

In the classroom, knowledge based on fact and for the acquisition of skills is emphasized, because it is more measurable by standardized tests. Dispositional knowledge (the kind which develops pupils' capacity to apply and live according to the moral and social theories they have learnt about) tends to rate a poor third, despite the rhetoric about education for citizenship.

The bureaucratic curriculum purchases concentration on a limited sphere of activity at the cost of making full use of the abilities and social sensitivities of teachers and pupils. Compliance can be reassuring. Giving priority to the core curriculum can protect teachers from worries about racial and religious disputes in the locality. In this model of school organization, unless the external managers agree that there is a problem and can tell the teachers how to solve it, then there is no problem.

MANAGING RE IN THE PRIMARY SCHOOL

In 1988 this approach had serious consequences for RE. Initially it was placed at the bottom of teachers' agenda, as there were no immediate guidelines or programmes to enact. The majority of primary schools appointed an RE curriculum co-ordinator and turned attention to National Curriculum Maths or Science, areas which threatened the subject competence of many staff. The way teachers became RE co-ordinators was indicative of teachers' thoughts on RE in 1988–89: 'You were away that day, so we gave the job to you'; 'We knew you went to church'; 'The probationer got the job because we won't have to publish results in RE'; 'This person is already very busy and won't be called on to do anything as RE co-ordinator until the LEA produces an Agreed Syllabus'.

When agreed syllabuses were published they tended to follow the pattern of National Curriculum core subjects' documents now familiar to teachers, offering programmes of study which highlighted Attainment Targets and indicated assessment procedures. As a result, RE was high on information but predictably low on dispositional knowledge, paying little attention to the strong feelings and attitudes which religious issues raise. Programmes of study lacked responsibility in that they raised awareness of the religious, ethnic and cultural differences without making it easier for pupils to handle the value conflicts evoked by contact with otherness. Sadly, recent Agreed RE Syllabuses for primary schools do not address the need to educate children to cope with the practical consequences of religious pluralism which the Swann Report emphasized and which Edward Hulmes had called for in 1979:

> Tolerance and understanding are insufficient even when elevated and institutionalised into an ideological commitment, in which the expression of respect for all traditions becomes the first clause in the new and universal creed, along with the denial of any exclusive body of absolute, revealed truth. One person is committed to a certain set of beliefs and values. Another is committed to a different set, and thus to a different course of action. In good faith (it is hoped) both are committed to conflicting and to possibly mutually destructive aims and ideals. A society which considers it proper to preserve the right of each to dissent from the others, and the right of others in their turn to disagree with basic issues of human existence, simply because these differences exist, has scarcely begun to take seriously any of the rival world views. Such a society may be deluded into thinking that it can survive the onslaught of what has recently been called 'a continuing dialectic of contraries'.[10]

A speech by the Chairman of the National Curriculum Council posed the RE quandary quite well. On 7 May 1992, David Pascall gave a speech to the Religious Education Council which confirmed an important curriculum place for RE. He emphasized RE's contribution, through moral education to the inculcation of 'respect for the laws and norms of society'. It had a particular part to play in a balanced curriculum which blended academic learning, the promotion of human values and encouragement to good behaviour.

These aspects of the speech reflected the approach of 'RE for social control' in the emphasis placed on the transmission of societal norms and approved behaviour. RE for behaviour modification may be socially useful in its emphasis on conformity but it runs counter to an exploration or appreciation of diversity. RE in this mode is a series of teacher exhortations to keep the rules and maintain good discipline. This may be spiced with stories, examples and role plays which invite pupils to identify the right way to behave in certain settings. Some of these are drawn from faith traditions so that correct behaviour comes with the favourable and powerful endorsement of a deity, whose earthly representative and interpreter is the teacher. Pupils quickly learn what are the right answers to moral questions for class-room purposes. However, they may be discriminating enough to know that turning the other cheek may not be a recipe for survival in the playground or park.

This approach has a limited effect on interpersonal behaviour, though it is effective in transmitting a language and set of rules about behaviour that teachers are required to pass on. In school, as in the wider world, these values are more honoured in talk than relational activity.

The emphasis on external constraints is congruent with the National Curriculum style. But it is strongly at odds with other themes in Pascall's speech.

1. He indicated awareness of recent clashes between contending religious and cultural traditions in Britain, referring to the *Satanic Verses* controversy.
2. He asked for a reinstatement of dispositional knowledge: 'How can schools help to develop in the young the will to do what is right?'
3. He called for schools to discuss the core values of education. Calling to mind his work at BP in introducing a set of core values, he commented,

> I find it ironic that an internationally competitive, commercial company like BP feels the need for core values whereas in the area where these issues are most important – the education of our children – we find they are considered too sensitive to talk about.[11]

Many teachers will find all of this challenging and refreshing. Response to the issues Pascall outlined calls for an extension of teacher skills which will delight many in the profession concerned about the de-skilling consequences of the Education Reform Act. It will certainly please the teacher who returned from an INSET day on the National Curriculum reciting a limerick to describe the teachers' lot:

> There once was a man who said, 'Damn,
> It's increasingly plain that I am
> A vehicle which moves
> In predestinate grooves.
> I'm not even a bus – I'm a tram.'

After a whole day of instruction on ATs and SATs and programmes of study, she saw herself delivering prepackaged English and Science units like an assistant in McDonald's serving up cheeseburgers and large fries, without even the promise of 'a nice day'.

The message is ambiguous. The fundamental shift in educational control over the last five years will make it difficult for teachers to discuss matters of educational principle and value. They have been told to 'deliver', not debate, the values already impressed in National Curriculum standing orders. This is a Catch-22 situation: 'Please be both A and not A in the exercise of your work.' One can only hope that teachers follow Rilke's advice to a young poet:

> Be patient towards all that is unresolved in your heart and try to love the contradictions themselves . . . Do not now seek the answers, that cannot be given because you would not be able to live them. Live the contradictions now. Perhaps you will then gradually, without noticing it, live along some distant day into the answer.[11]

A future resolution is unlikely to be based upon a controlling management style which filters out contradictions.

School management which is adept at survival and development in an unstable environment needs teachers with reflective and coping skills, not teachers wholly possessed by anxiety about immediate external demands. In contrast to 'controlling' tendencies, the hallmarks of 'coping' are respect for the natural variety of things, connectedness to the context, and non-reliance upon fixed rules, methods or techniques.

Management for controlling

* Rooted in images from the mechanical and technical world
* Believes that technology can change anything in an organization
* Works through the enforcement of routines and procedures
* Reduces everything to parts
* Concerned with costs
* Hierarchical
* Uses power
* Edits and administers the world

Management for coping

* Rooted in images from the natural world
* Believes that ecological balance must be maintained between an organization and its environment
* Works through flexible and mutative understanding and interactions
* Emphasizes wholes
* Concerned with values
* Collaborative
* Uses authority
* Encourages connections between elements in the world

The 'coping' approach stands in opposition to the technological creed which believes all things – whether values, teachers or pupil – are malleable and can change shape or purpose. It is especially appropriate for RE since it is distinguished by gracious and respectful relations with 'the other'. Insofar as this is achieved, 'coping' strategies are ecologically sound educational management practices, for they understand that action which deforms or denies 'the other' reduces the quality of life of everyone in the school and threatens the harmony and justice of wider society. A style of managing informed by these principles is paradoxically able to value the particular and distinctive as well as having a regard for the integrated wholeness of its environment.

COLLABORATION AND COPING

'Coping management' requires the commitment and participation of all teaching staff. A collaborative context facilitates the development of a sustaining vision for which all are accountable. It also provides pupils with positive examples of adult co-operation. Official policy over the years has come to support participative approaches to school management.

> The professionalism of the teacher also involves playing a part in the corporate develop-ment of the school. HMI reports frequently refer to the importance of professional team work, where the teachers within a school agree together on the overall goals of the school, on the policies for the curriculum in the widest sense, including policies for the standard of behaviour expected of pupils and for the relationship expected between teacher and pupils. The pupils' own ability to co-operate and work well with each other is enhanced by the experience of members of staff working productively together in a professional relationship.[12]

But such co-operation involves risk and uncertainty. Not everyone feels competent to deal with the secret variety of philosophy and practice which a staff group hides from itself. Issues of redeployment, early retirement, school closure, opting out, budgeting, teacher appraisal and the National Curriculum conspire to create an atmosphere non-conducive to fluid and participative practices.

The school does not run like clockwork. It maybe more accurately thought of as a sea: at times tempestuous, sometimes placid, which hides peculiar tidal drifts from the unsuspecting. Working in this fluid environment it is helpful if the staff of a school, like the crew of a boat, have charted a common course. This is essential if all facets of the curriculum, not only RE, have to attend to the spiritual and moral development of pupils.

Part Two of this book provides a theoretical framework to support staff groups wishing to explore collaboration as a key to the effective handling of RE in the primary school. But before that is offered, it is necessary to explore the factors in school life which work against the recognition of pluralism and pluriformity. Unless we accurately identify and understand the ways in which avoidance of differences is almost 'soldered' into primary school life, exhortations to change will only be so much hot air.

NOTES AND REFERENCES

1. *The Complete Poems of Emily Dickinson*, edited by T. H. Johnson (1970) (London: Faber & Faber), pp. 416–17.
2. M. Buber (1961) *Between Man and Man*, translated by R. Gregor Smith (London: Fontana), pp. 22–3.
3. The Runnymede Trust (1985) *Education for All: A Summary of the Swann Report on the Education of Ethnic Minority Children* (London: DES/HMSO), p. 1.
4. Swann *et al.* (1985) *Education for All: The Report of the Committee of Inquiry into the Education of Children from Ethnic Minority Groups* (London: DES/HMSO), p. 321.
5. *Ibid.*, p. 475.
6. *Ibid.*, p. 508.
7. A. D. Gilbert (1980) *The Making of Post-Christian Britain* (London: Longman), p. 94.
8. M. W. Apple and S. Junck (1992) 'You don't have to be a teacher to teach this unit: Teaching, technology and control in the classroom', in A. Hargreaves and M. G. Fullan

(eds), *Understanding Teacher Development* (New York: Teachers' College Press), pp. 23–4.

9.   C. Aitken Handy (1986) *Understanding Schools as Organizations* (London: Penguin), p. 94.

10.   E. Hulmes (1979) *Commitment and Neutrality in Religious Education* (London: Geoffrey Chapman), pp. 34–5.

11.   D. Pascall, Speech to the Religious Education Council, 7 May 1992.

12.   R. M. Rilke (1963) *Letters to a Young Poet*, translated by M. D. Herter (New York: W. W. Norton), p. 33.

12.   DES (1985) *Better Schools* (London: HMSO), p. 35.

Chapter 3

Difference and Primary School Culture

He is quick, thinking in clear images;
I am slow, thinking in broken images.

He becomes dull, trusting to his clear images;
I become sharp, mistrusting my broken images.

Trusting his images, he assumes their relevance;
Mistrusting my images, I question their relevance.

Assuming their relevance, he assumes the fact;
Questioning their relevance, I question the fact.

When the fact fails him, he questions his senses;
When the fact fails me, I approve my senses.

He continues quick and dull in his clear images;
I continue slow and sharp in my broken images.

He in a new confusion of his understanding;
I in a new understanding of my confusion.

Robert Graves, 'In Broken Images'[1]

Each primary school has a particular ethos and atmosphere which distinguishes it from every other. This uniqueness is a source of pride to staff and pupils and is celebrated in customs, festivals and practices not found elsewhere. The recognition of this variety in the school scene gives substance to the concept of parental choice in education. Schools are now being asked to offer parents school mission statements which make their values and priorities clear. Production of these documents requires that teachers explore together the lived values and vision which guides their work and distinguishes it from that done in other primary schools in the locality.

The difference between schools is keenly felt by anyone who has cause to go into a number of them. Places have different smells, receive visitors differently, foster differing relational styles and give evidence of different educational priorities. Acknowledgement of this variety does not imply that they defy comparison or have nothing in common. Each school is delegated to perform the task of the education of young children. To achieve this, all use methods and curriculum designs informed by educational legislation, research, ideology and received wisdom. The ingredients of the school cocktail are common, it is the mix that gives a distinctive flavour.

This chapter explores nine aspects of primary practice and demonstrates that problems with pluralism are inevitable, given the basic assumptions of infant and junior schools. Table 3.1 on page 31 provides an overview of the arguments and conclusions presented.

1. CONCERN WITH ORDER

Primary schools are rightly concerned with order. The school offers its pupils the security of a reliable and structured environment which offers the possibility of stable relationships with a set of trustworthy adults. In spite of all evidence to the contrary human endeavours are based on a belief in the essential orderliness of things. This helps people to develop comfortable routines which only rarely become so rigidly obsessional as to be dysfunctional. Teachers strive to develop organizational abilities, rules and practices which will enable classes of young children to learn together. They like to be prepared for every situation and fear being in a classroom where chaos reigns.

All people have days when nothing planned actually gets done. At such times human beings are absorbed into an internal world of amorphous half-perceptions, without structure or direction. These fruitless and frightening hours are reminders that undifferentiated chaos lurks below the regular patternings of focused consciousness. In the light of such intimations from the psyche one can readily understand the tight management strategy described by one headteacher.

'I have a particular thing that I want to concentrate on every year. We really get to grips with that and when we've got it sorted out, we'll move on and target something else for the next year.'

(Fieldnote, George Street)

This is a simple and appealing approach to school organization but it has inadequacies. It is built on the assumption that conclusions reached and decisions taken about school policy and practice in one year will retain their relevance over a period of successive years regardless of changes in pupil numbers, staffing or national educational policy.

The consequence of this management strategy is the artificial separation of issues on the school agenda. This discourages staff from making new connections to matters which have already been closed, settled and organized. In the face of such order it becomes increasingly difficult to make changes to curriculum practice or raise questions of ethos when

'we already settled that three years ago. It's not relevant to our discussion here.'

(Fieldnote, Richmond Road)

2. THE MAINTENANCE OF GOOD RELATIONS

Editing or ignoring the contributions of colleagues in staff meetings is guaranteed to arouse strong feelings between people and lead to friction. It poses a threat to the existence of pleasant and orderly staff relations. This is anathema in the primary school, which places a high premium on good relationships between people whether staff or pupils. Activities and talk in class-room and staffroom tend to be structured to avoid emotional displays which could fuel interpersonal conflict.

> Sustaining the school milieu is one of the most important aspects of the informal accoun-
> tability system which governs teachers' behaviour . . . The essential minimum contribution
> of every teacher is the maintenance of a state of peaceful coexistence . . . A teacher and
> the pupils should not disturb the peace within the school . . . A teacher's pupils should
> not be ill-mannered or have unusual work habits that make them difficult for others to
> teach . . . A teacher should not threaten the autonomy of other teachers.[2]

This ground rule finds its own justification in individual schools.

> 'There's not enough room to swing a cat in the staffroom here. And it's used as a secretary's office
> . . . It's twelve years since there was a new staff member appointed apart from the Head. So the five
> of us have been together for twelve years . . . You get to know everybody's hobby horses and the
> things they are really touchy about. Over the years we've developed an unspoken understanding of
> the things we really disagree about. I suppose we have a pact to avoid them for the sake of keeping
> the peace. You can't afford to fall out when you all have to share such a small space.'
>
> (Fieldnote, Ryesdon C of E)

This attitude prevents staff caught in this bind from addressing many matters related to values or commitments for fear of revealing deeply held differences amongst them-selves. Behind the apologia for the bland is the suspicion that the school is a fragile organization which could be blown apart by violent disagreement.

Staff know that they need the support of their peers to survive stressful times.

> 'Let's face it, you've got to get on together. You need the others when you come back into the staf-
> froom after a bad morning . . . We all get on well, even if there is the odd person you don't like too
> much . . . We have a laugh. You have to, if you're going to stay sane.'
>
> (Fieldnote, St Clare's RC)

The pressure to maintain good relationships can lead to an unspoken collusion to avoid contentious professional issues.

> Insensitivity to the value dimension of the teaching task may be nourished by the profes-
> sional climate of schools . . . One of the most pervasive elements in the culture and one
> which characterises many other educational institutions, is the assumption of value con-
> sensus on key educational and institutional issues, where, even if dissent is not actually sup-
> pressed, the civilized rejoinder 'But that's a values question' is not so much a statement of
> fact, as a device for curtailing discussion before it becomes uncomfortably divergent.[3]

A consensus about values is uneasily assumed on the understanding that nothing is allowed to test it. In an organization based on personal relations there can be no such thing as a professional disagreement, but it may be unwise to assume consensus or prac-tical activity arising from proclaimed policy.

3. VOCATIONALISM

Confusion between the personal and the professional tends to be found in any occupational area described as a vocation. In teaching this vocation is seen as a professional expression of a personal ability to relate to children and understand their needs. In a staffroom full of people who all relate well to children and know their needs it will be difficult to have a professional debate on children's relational and learning needs. Questions posed relating to any individual's contribution could be taken as a great professional and personal insult. The fear of bruising sensitivities in this way is very strong, as teachers' emotional investment in their work is very high. Though there is precious little in documents from the DES, HMI and SEAC about emotion, school life is characterized by feelings and occasionally hurt feelings. If the professional is seen as the personal and the personal can't be probed because it's tied up with an individual's identity and self-worth, then there is an effective embargo on professional debate.

But the personal is a two-edged sword. It is so powerful it cannot be investigated. However, individual contributions to a curriculum development exercise are often made with a reticence which indicates professional insecurity.

> 'How do I know what I'm saying is right? I haven't read everything. I don't really know. When it comes down to it we are just sitting around trading opinions. We need an expert to tell us what is really right.'
>
> *(Fieldnote, St Benedict's RC)*

Such remarks come from a belief that somewhere there is one absolute, objective viewpoint, a god's eye-view of each situation, unimpeded by personal history and partialities. This is a myth but it is widespread.

> So long as I keep before me an ideal of an absolute observer, of knowledge in the absence of any viewpoint, I can only see my situation as being a source of error. But once I have acknowledged that through it I am geared to all actions and all knowledge that are meaningful to me, then my contact with the social in the finitude of my situation is revealed to me as the starting point of all truth.[4]

In the absence of this insight the individual's contribution is trivialized. It is as if nothing said could be regarded as valuable, because it was not everything.

Professional development work can raise the personal sensitivies of staff. Whilst taking part in an exercise 'What is religion?' in an RE INSET programme a teacher objected:

> 'I didn't come here for this. This RE course is supposed to be about what I do with my junior class. You should be telling me what I have to say to them. This is adult Religious Education. If I wanted to think about religion I'd go to see my own minister. INSET after school is not meant to play about with people's private and personal religious views.'
>
> *(Fieldnote, Ryesdon, C of E)*

In 1974 Witkin issued a warning about the high price of children's learning. It may be even more relevant in relation to staff. He points out that there is

> a world that exists only because the individual exists. It is the world of his own sensations and feelings . . . If the price of finding oneself in the world is that of losing the world in oneself, then the price is more than anyone can afford.[5]

The implications of Laurence Stenhouse's dictum 'personal development precedes curriculum development' is apparent in this context. It is clear that attempts to introduce social changes through educational initiatives, such as multicultural education, peace studies, world studies, anti-racism, multifaith approaches to RE, and sex education, are largely determined by individual teachers' preparedness to risk a review of their own life assumptions.

4.   LACK OF CLEAR AIMS

The inability to name or permit development of personal attitudes means that discussions about educational aims are destined to be few and far between. Aims are concerned with a long-term vision which entices an enterprise forward, forever eluding final realization. They are meant to provoke the imagination and inspire, but are doomed to cause frustration in a time more concerned with the achievement of short-term goals. The challenge of aims is likely then to be replaced by pre-set targets and objectives thought to be attainable.

This diluted approach to managing policy is designed to bolster a sense of competence and capability in a school staff at a time when outsiders require demonstrable and quantifiable indicators of progress and success. Staff meetings convened in this atmosphere tend to be about immediate objectives and focus on the administration of events. Planning is reduced to the order of 'Are the buses booked?' or 'When do you want the grids completed?' rather than a pedagogical exploration of the curriculum rationale for proposed activity. The emphasis placed on assessment in the last few years has led to schools losing sight of the larger social aims of education emphasized in the Schools Council Primary Aims Project of 1975. It is as if teachers and schools can only demonstrate efficiency and efficacy by reducing the scope of their activities and intentions.

Other strains in the ideology of primary education which contribute to the fog about aims were described by W. Taylor in 1969 as

> rejection of pluralism: suspicion of the intellect and the intellectual; a lack of interest in
> political and structural change, a stress upon the intuitive and the intangible; upon spon-
> taneity and creativity . . . a hunger for the satisfactions of interpersonal life within the
> community and the small group and a flight from rationality.[6]

This may reflect the way in which the Plowden Report was taken up by schools to form a professional consensus based on 'childcentredness'. But it remains a significant aspect of ideology today. What this approach lacks in analysis it makes up for in jargon: 'Children learn to write by writing'; 'Experience not curriculum'; 'The child not the curriculum'; 'Learning not teaching'. But the security of shared aphorisms is no replacement for a comprehensive dialogue on the theory which informs teacher activity and stimulates pupils to learn. The introduction of National Curriculum Attainment Targets and assessment procedures which some hoped would increase teacher reflection can work to short-circuit clarification of curriculum aims, diverting attention to mandated objectives.

Neither aims nor objectives were a high priority for the teacher who spent an INSET session cutting and pasting a display of pupils' work whilst colleagues laboured to devise shared aims for a programme of study on Ramadan. She explained that she had better things to do with her time than talk a lot of theory.

> 'I only value INSET work that gives me an activity I can do the next day with my class . . . But I'll just row in with anything you decide.'
>
> *(Fieldnote, Hill View)*

Her behaviour indicates the activism which plays a large part in primary ideology. Busy teachers and busy pupils are the indicators of good practice. Busy about what and to what end are not recognized as real questions. This denigration of talk is a major obstacle to professional dialogue, without which there can be neither development nor implementation of policy.

The real work of the staff as a group is talk. Without a common language, shared priorities and curricular strategies the whole staff cannot work together. If the group is unprepared for the struggle towards shared understanding, issues will always be fudged. This guarantees a peaceful life, as no one will be called upon to examine or explain their professional assumptions or behaviours.

5. TRADITION

Allowing things to roll on without close scrutiny is often justified by an appeal to tradition. The argument for inherited attitudes and practices gets a sympathetic hearing in school circles. Much of the curriculum and its methods of transmission are the fruit of received wisdom. Stress within the school on the conservation and communication of this legacy of skills and values has its place. But teachers can get stuck in a time warp, labelling educational initiatives as new-fangled gimmicks when they may meet pupils' needs.

Investment in the past can go hand in hand with a suspicion of the new and fear of the future. If children are to be prepared to live in the future they must have resources that differ from those given to their forebears. What was good enough for their parents may not be adequate to their needs. The problem of developing tradition asserts itself most strongly when the offer of something different is interpreted as a criticism of the practices of previous generations.

Voluntary aided schools can find themselves in this situation with regard to changing practices in Religious Education. This can be seen in sharp focus in an incident in a Roman Catholic primary school:

> 'The class 6 teacher has been told to take down the displays made by pupils which show the religious symbols of the main faith traditions of the world. The priest who is the chairman of governors does not think that they have any place in the school. He says that the pupils may be confused by knowledge of false religions.'
>
> *(Fieldnote, St Peter's RC)*

6.   THE INFLUENCE OF EXTERNAL AGENCIES

The example above indicates that activities in school are influenced by other institutions and social forces. This makes education a political matter in every understanding of the word. The parliamentary conflict surrounding educational legislation such as the Education Reform Act of 1988 provides an example of the politics of education, understood in its most literal terms. However, rows about who has the authority to determine school activity take place at other levels.

Diocesan policy on admissions to church schools may restrict access to one racial or cultural group, thereby affecting the pupil population of neighbouring county maintained schools. Entry to popular church schools can be used as a recruitment device for church members. Changes in housing policy and employment opportunities may lead to unstable pupil numbers. Changes in the ethnicity of inner-city inhabitants can lead to voluntary aided foundations, both Roman Catholic and Church of England, serving a Muslim and Hindu pupil population. Parental disaffection expressed through those who wait at the school gates can also exert strong influence in the running of the school. These external pressures give some idea of the competing interests which seek to influence school direction.

Since these interest groups always exist, the professional expert authority of staff is under constant pressure from sectional interests in society. It is not only that education is too important to leave to the teachers'. Teachers are not in control of community happenings which impact on schools and the people inside them.

7.   LACK OF CULTURAL ANALYSIS

As educational institutions are buffeted by and responsive to changes in their environment it seems logical that teachers would be keen to analyse developments in society. But the majority of primary staff groups are remarkable for their lack of social and cultural enquiry. Central to this is the desire to avoid differences of opinion among the staff. Teachers are members of society, formed and filled by attitudes, political and religious beliefs, cultural tastes and prejudices. Social and cultural analysis would enable the staff to identify resources to help pupils learn, but it could also cause disputes over the value assumptions which underpin each teacher's practice.

Value issues are the dynamite which can blow apart staff cohesion. The pretence that education is value-free springs not so much from acceptance of a particular philosophy, as a collusion to preserve peace among colleagues. But a coherent curriculum cannot be created by ignoring these differences.

> Cultural analysis for curriculum purposes is extremely difficult and fraught with the risk of accusations of value bias. On the other hand, ignoring value issues will not banish them and the teacher who argues 'We must not impose our values on the children' displays not so much neutrality, as professional self-deception.[7]

Schools defend themselves against the threat of disruptive variety beyond the school gates by acting as if there was a rigid separation between school and world. This supports the fantasy that in the cross-over from one to another an invisible screen filters out of educational participants all preferences, history and particularities. The school is then protected from the alien influences and demands of a world out there. Focus shifts to the needs of the child. Plowden emphasized that 'At the heart of education lies the child' whose education required 'sensitive nurture'. This romantic language fosters an image of the school as a maternal cradle, a womb even, definitely something separate from a hostile world. This special world also encloses the staff in a protected environment, innocent of the ways of the world.

The real world then becomes a resource for interesting factual information which can broaden the horizons of the child. Culture, in any of its aspects – material, artistic, spiritual, intellectual or ritual – is plundered to offer items for neutral observation.

> 'Some of the staff are keen that the pupils learn "the basic facts" of three or four world religions. They believe that learning about many will reduce the likelihood of preaching any faith in particular. Some like this approach because it is readily assessable.'
>
> *(Fieldnote, Richmond Road)*

Culture may not be analysed by staff but it is raided by teachers to furnish interesting things to know about.

8. THE IMPORTANCE OF RIGHT ANSWERS

The imparting of facts is grist to the mill of schools, which are pressured for time in which to make a demonstrable difference to their pupils. Pleasing Mr Gradgrind becomes a shadowy sub-agenda of the school.

> Now, what I want is facts. Teach these boys and girls nothing but facts. Facts alone are what is wanted in life.[8]

John Holt sees the seductiveness of this approach.

> Practically everything we do in school tends to make children answer-centred. In the first place, right answers pay off. Schools are a kind of temple of worship for 'right answers' and the way to get ahead is to lay a lot of them on the altar. In the second place, the chances are good that teachers themselves are answer-centred certainly in mathematics, but by no means only there. What they do, they do because this is what the book says to do, or what they have always done. In the third place, even those teachers who are not themselves answer-centred will probably not see, as for many years I did not, the distinction between problem-centredness and answer-centredness, far less understand its importance.[9]

Education as the quest for right answers encourages pupils to develop a view of the world based on 'one-right-wayism'. This is a world-view which believes that there is only one right way to be/do a task or to think. It is profoundly dualistic and reduces the likelihood of ever respecting the different ideas and practices of others.

A world where things are either right or wrong is one of minimal uncertainty and is easily regulated, but a curriculum based upon it is unbalanced and has no place for pluralism. This weakens the quality of children's learning and does not do justice to the scope of their imaginations or the nuances of life enjoyed by teachers and pupils in classrooms.

9. CHANGE OVERLOAD

Since the Education Reform Act schools have been bombarded with a stream of legis-
lative demands for change. The introduction of the National Curriculum, Attainment
Targets, testing of pupils, evaluation of teachers, local management of schools (LMS),
opting out and the new responsibilities of governing bodies has left schools reeling from
the rapid pace of change. Reports of stress and the fall in the number of applications
for primary headships tell a tale of change overload.

It is not surprising that pluralism and cultural diversity is played down in the face of
more immediate priorities set by central government. The pressures to meet the new
demands cause a narrowing of educational horizons so that staff can channel their
energies into specific tasks and projects which will then be evaluated as part of their own
appraisal procedure.

Perhaps the vexed issue of difference is ordained to take a back seat until failure
to take it seriously is recognized as the root of many educational and managerial
problems.

GROUND WORK FOR CHANGE

The nine highlighted factors in primary education (see Table 3.1) militate against the
recognition of difference as an important issue. Behind each factor identified lies a fear
of, or a desire to protect, some dynamic in present experience. This works to prevent
development. New ways of being and behaving depend upon questioning these elements
in primary school culture. This requires anxiety-reducing strategies which encourage
teachers to deal with pluralism more coherently in staffroom and class-room.

There are nine important changes in thinking which need to be made before teachers
will be able to grasp the nettle of difference.

1. The obsession with control and order needs to be replaced with an ability to
   make new connections between existing elements of experience. This would
   provide a new basis for understanding changing situations.
2. The fear that interpersonal conflict will result from plurality of values and
   commitments needs to be replaced by a discovery of security at the heart of
   working relations born out of use of diverse staff resources.
3. The confusion of the personal and the professional worlds which 'vocationalism'
   encourages needs to be replaced by a clearer understanding of the role of the
   teacher.
4. The lack of clarity about aims which muddies questions of success or failure
   needs to be replaced by regular staff discussion which has a common focus.
5. The emphasis placed on received wisdom and tradition needs to be balanced
   by a concern for continual renewal in school. This would prevent the
   myopia which sees no problems unless they are capable of solution by old
   methods.
6. Teacher concern about the power of external agents in directing school policy
   needs to be influenced by an appraisal of the limits and possibilities of their own
   authority.

Table 3.1

Key factors in primary school life	Underlying issues	Consequences for difference	Prerequisites for change
1. Concern with order	Fear of chaos	Differences are disruptive. They disturb the status quo.	School staff to make new connections
2. Maintenance of good relations	Fear of strong feelings and interpersonal conflict	Differences should not be explored. When strong feelings are engaged the unity of the school is put at risk.	Secure working relations among the staff to use the plurality of the values and commitments as resources
3. Vocationalism	Confusion about the personal and the professional	Differences are subsumed by professional commonalities which are seen as more significant. Professional development is resisted if it conflicts with personal convictions.	Staff to clarify the connections and separations in their personal and professional worlds
4. Lack of clarity about aims	Cultural confusion	Differences are fudged. A discussion of aims would surface unexamined assumptions for investigation.	The work of school staff to have a common focus
5. Tradition	Concern for the value of received wisdom	Differences pose questions about inherited practices and attitudes.	Continual renewal in schools
6. Influence of external agencies	Concern that 'Education is too important to leave to teachers'	Differences arising from conflicts about power and authority are structured into the politics of the school	Staff to recognize and explore the possibilities and limitations of their authority
7. Lack of cultural analysis	Reticence in making value judgements explicit	Differences of custom, race, morals and religion are seen as cultural curios.	A framework to assist professional discourse on the educational environment
8. The importance of right answers	Desire to minimalize uncertainity	Difference and variety of cultural and religious practices undermines 'one-right-wayism'	Staff to have the freedom to re-think and 'unknow'
9. Change overload	Stress produced by demands for a rapid response	Differences are ignored in the face of 'greater priorities'	Time for staff to come to terms with developments

7. The reticence in making value judgements explicit needs to be overcome by the development of frameworks and structures for professional discussion of the cultural milieu of education.
8. The quest for certainty which limits imagination and educational choice needs to be abandoned in favour of managerial space to rethink and 'unknow' some aspects of school life.
9. The pressure to produce a response to today's changes by yesterday needs to be resisted, so that staff have time to come to terms with the implications of developments.

These recommendations may find favour with teachers who recognize themselves trapped into counter-productive ways of thinking and acting.

'I wish we weren't so sensitive and suspicious. Some of the social situations facing us really need a lot of talking about. We don't do that talking and say it's because of time, but really we know that the staff is divided into splinter groups and separate camps about lots of things. So we say nothing and just roll along. In a big school it's easy to do.'

(Fieldnote, Richmond Road)

'I'd like to think that we [the staff] had a part to play in managing the school. But we get so tied up with our own class that we are happy to let the Head make the decisions. So we end up doing things we don't approve of. It's our own fault really.'

(Fieldnote, George Street)

The road to educational reform is piled high with recommendations no one could act on and needs that remained unmet. The real art of any programme of educational change is its rootedness in a theory and strategy which enables people to adopt new behaviours, attitudes and ways of thinking and relating.

The field of Group Relations provides relevant theoretical and analytic insights to address issues of change and diversity within the educational system. This inter-disciplinary field aims to increase the ability of people to form work groups committed to the performance of defined tasks. It does this by placing the emphasis on

1.   factors in the environment which affect the work task;
2.   factors in the psychic life of the work group which influence the task in hand.

In this attempt to hold together the political environment and the emotional life of a group as it undertakes work, Group Relations aims to understand and interpret, integrate and organize fragments of lived behaviour, events and attitudes into intelligibly patterned wholes. In this way a group can examine and alter its policies or working methods. The approach relies on a combination of insights drawn from psychoanalytic thinking and systems theory.

In Part Two these complementary theories are described. Insights and working methods are presented to illuminate the difficulties experienced by nine staff groups undertaking RE development work.

NOTES AND REFERENCES

1.   *Collected Poems* (1975) (London: Cassell), p. 80.
2.   T. Becher, M. R. Eraut and J. Knight (1981) *Policies for Educational Accountability* (London: Heinemann), p. 61.
3.   R. J. Alexander (1984) *Primary Teaching* (London: Cassell), p. 121.
4.   M. Merleau Ponty (1962) *Phenomenology of Perception*, translated by Colin Smith (London: Routledge & Kegan Paul), p. 142.
5.   F. Witkin (1974) *The Intelligence of Feeling* (London: Heinemann), p. 94.
6.   W. Taylor (1969) *Society and the Education of Teachers* (London: Faber & Faber), p. 12.
7.   R. J. Alexander, *Primary Teaching*, p. 32.
8.   C. Dickens (1969) *Hard Times* (London: Penguin) (first published 1854).
9.   J. Holt (1964) *How Children Fail* (New York: Dell), p. 90.

Part Two

New Perspectives

This section introduces Group Relations as a useful perspective for understanding and analysing the dynamics of collaborative work in schools. Chapter 6 introduces the work of an RE curriculum development project which employed this conceptual framework in its consultancy to nine primary schools.

New Perspectives

Chapter 4

The Emotional Dynamic of the Group

I promise to make you more alive than you've ever been.
For the first time you'll see your pores opening
like the gills of fish and you'll hear
the noise of blood in galleries
and feel light gliding on your corneas
like the dragging of a dress across the floor.
For the first time, you'll note gravity's prick
like a thorn in your heel,
and your shoulder blades will hurt from the imperative of wings.
I promise to make you so alive that
the fall of dust on furniture will deafen you,
and you'll feel your eyebrows like two wounds forming
and your memories will seem to begin
with the creation of the world.

Nina Cassian, 'Ordeal'[1]

Learning and consciousness-raising have much in common. Both can be a bit of an ordeal. People who work in schools sometimes complain that life there can be stressful. The demands of last-minute rehearsals for the play, an impending inspection, the loss of valued colleagues, or running tests for 7-year-olds alongside a normal teaching schedule cause real strain. In times of pressure people see themselves required to do, provide or produce ideas, materials or solutions to problems, while suspecting that they cannot muster adequate resources of time, competence or energy to do so. If such experiences are of relatively short duration and an infrequent occurence staff ride out the rough times purposeful and in fairly good humour. Prolonged periods of stress take their toll in ill health and a decline in enthusiasm and capacity for work. Despite indications to the contrary in the growth of the stress management and counselling industry, there is no universal panacea for knotted stomachs, raised blood pressure and jangled nerve endings in the workplace.

BIOLOGY AND INSECURITY

The biology that twentieth-century human beings share with their cave-dwelling ancestors is adapted to ensure survival in encounters with strong or fast predators. Though we live in a technological age our automatic response system and body chemistry are designed to compel us to fight or run away from that which looks threatening. Identifying a stimulus to action, the body pumps adrenalin, blood flow to the extremities increases fleetness of foot and power in the punch, and blood pressure and heartrate rise. This helped the hunter surprised by a bear to muster all his resources for attack or flight. After running a safe distance into the hills his body would relax, resuming a normal physiological condition.

For the headteacher responding to falling rolls in an inner-city school or the teacher who discovers racist and feuding factions in the class-room, these physiological reactions are less immediately useful. The person is geared up for instant action, when any instant response will be woefully inadequate. The process of handling stressful concerns over a long period can cause the body to maintain a chemical and biological state damaging to its own immune system. Unlike the hunter who enjoys deep and restful sleep after telling the glorious tale of the defeat or evasion of the bear, educational professionals are kept awake by their concerns. Undischarged stress becomes compounded by tiredness and each day is increasingly difficult to survive, let alone organize.

If our species is biologically ill-equipped to deal with threatening relational and institutional issues, then the make-up for our psyche, established in infancy, seems correspondingly primitive. The human species has no special mental facility whereby its adults can cope with the anxieties of life. We arrive in life screaming at the terrors of an alien environment, with a tendency to construe subsequent situations of stress and change in similar life-threatening terms. The infant survives because of its howling ability to convey intolerance of hunger, cold and loneliness to a responsive mother who can change every situation for the better. She is the benevolent source of all gratification but is also the origin of all frustration; providing or denying food, and responsible for changes in temperature. This early experience of ambiguity intimates that the reality of the world is a paradoxical compound of the pleasant and the unpleasant. It sets the human life agenda of coping with self and the world in terms of contending destructive and constructive forces.

Since humankind cannot bear too much reality, life is lived commuting between two worlds, the real and the fantasy. In more sophisticated stress-free times people live in a complex world of ambiguity, where nuances resonate and all motives, especially one's own, are suspect. When the anxiety level climbs all have recourse to the magical black-and-white world constructed in early childhood, where life is simple, we are totally virtuous and all evil resides in our designated enemies. This is the oscillation of adult life. It is one device in an array of learned strategies which help to preserve personal comfort in the face of anxieties.

INSECURITY, ENERGY AND WORK

Acknowledged or not, eruptions from the unconscious touch all aspects of every work setting. The opportunity for purposeful action in the world is also an occasion for potential failure. People fear the loss of personal esteem and organize work demands into reassuring patterns of replicable activities and relations.

The dynamics of the working environment are not adequately understood by seeing work only as a rational construction for task achievement. Ritual procedures and structures are developed in the workplace to keep distressing feelings of insecurity at bay. In the long-term these defences against anxiety may actually prove unhelpful to the overall objectives of an organization. But they may be retained and endowed with a symbolic significance because they are a reminder of a valued former identity. They are the organizational equivalent of security blankets.

In school life they could perhaps take the form of reluctance to alter a class-room layout which impedes group work, or an insistence on triple mounting of pupils' work despite straightened school finances. Such incongruities signal worry in the face of change. Human beings have a rich repertoire of defences. Table 4.1 outlines a variety of strategies used to repress and displace anxiety.

If the source of discomfort is located in the self, the threat can be externalized and projected onto a threatening enemy.

> If one remembers that on the whole the ego is better prepared by experience and practice to deal with external dangers, it is easy to see why projection is such a prevalent defence. By fabricating a 'real' enemy, the person feels adequate to take command of the situation. He can, for example, destroy or attempt to destroy his enemy. This allows him to satisfy his aggressive impulse without incurring a feeling of shame. For this reason, projection is probably the most effective of the defence mechanisms.[2]

Effective or not, all these defences eat up energy. The weariness brought about by repelling or repressing unpleasant aspects of reality reduces personal capacity for fruitful action. Mental energy generated by the instincts is a finite resource. Investing energy in

Table 4.1

The human personality is shaped as the psyche learns to cope with raw desires and impulses. As the person matures these are controlled or relegated to the unconscious, along with painful memories and traumas. The adult keeps their threatened eruption at bay by using defence mechanisms. Freud and others have described the following defences against anxiety.

Repression:	pushing down rejected ideas and impulses into the unconscious
Displacement:	redirecting impulses aroused by one person or situation onto another target
Denial:	refusal to recognize an impulse evoking feeling, memory or fact
Fixation:	rigid commitment to an attitude or behaviour
Idealization:	emphasizing the positive aspects of a person or situation to protect oneself from the negative
Projection:	attributing one's own feelings and desires to another, e.g. I don't like him because he doesn't like me
Regression:	reducing present demands on the ego by escaping into childhood behaviour
Introjection:	taking into the psyche aspects of the world
Sublimation:	redirecting basic impulses into socially approved expression
Rationalization:	the development of complicated rationals to mask the dubious motivation of intentions or actions
Splitting:	dividing elements of experience in a dualistic way to deny the ambigious nature of reality

anxiety-reducing processes means that there is less available for productive activity. If energy is needed to recognize an uncomfortable feeling, more is required to repress it and more still to maintain its repression. Such improvidence leads to a situation where normal reality-based activities can no longer be accomplished because energy is being drained in a vampire-like way to support a false perspective.

The work world is always making new demands which appear threatening at first. The emergence of a pluralistic society exerts pressure for development in educational skills and practice. Schools staff can run from these challenges or waste energy on projecting aggression and animosity onto an imagined enemy who is blamed for the disturbance. It would be more useful to reclaim the energy currently used to fend off fear and address that fear directly.

The anxiety that staff and schools may be incapable of development can only be dealt with by thoughtful and purposefully structured task activity. The ideal work situation involves an accurate perception of external reality and an understanding of the unconscious psychic dynamics of those doing the work. It is a productive alliance of thought and feeling.

During the last war William Bion became interested in the way in which mental energy could be used in co-operative working groups. His ideas throw light on those occasions when emotional and relational involvement in the dynamics of the workplace supersede the work task itself.

BION AND ANXIETY

William Bion had been a tank commander during World War I and in World Ward II had responsibility for identifying men with leadership potential. He also worked for a while in Northfield hospital, running a military psychiatric facility for battle fatigued troops. The unit suffered from low morale, dirty wards and a pervasive atmosphere of apathy. To make matters worse, Bion himself was beseiged by administrative problems which he later came to recognize as the neurotic problems of the unit expressed in organizational terms.

He experimented to improve the situation by working psychologically within the military framework. He aimed to restore discipline by harnessing the energies of the men in a fight against the common enemy, 'the existence of neurosis as a disability of the community'. As there was a common problem, the activities of each section were organized so that members worked collectively to defeat it.

All the men joined groups so that everyone had a purpose, whether that was making baskets or learning to read maps. A compulsory daily parade developed into a plenary group meeting where the business of the unit could be openly discussed. As the capacity for reflection on their own activity increased the men took more initiatives, morale improved and there was greater concern for the cleanliness of the unit. Now there was a recognizable *esprit de corps*. Bion saw the changes as evidence of the soldiers' increasing capacity to get in touch with reality, form relationships amongst themselves, and work effectively together on a shared task.

This working method lasted for only six weeks but Bion's later work develops the principles which emerged from Northfield.

1. Individual behaviour influences and is influenced by the behaviour of other members of the group.
2. The emotions and anxious feelings of group members have a great impact on the relational work and task attainment of the group. If this fact is not recognized then the group can be controlled by its unconscious anxieties and mental energy is squandered.
3. Problems of administration and management are personal and interpersonal problems expressed in organizational terms.
4. Groups develop when they learn from their own experience of achieving and maintaining contact with reality.

BION AND GROUP BEHAVIOUR

In later years Bion continued his work with groups by adopting the role of consultant to group behaviour and process in other contexts. He directed his attention to the group as a whole focusing on behaviour which indicated its shared anxieties and illusions. He was able to distinguish two distinct modes of behaviour in any group which indicated its shared anxieties and illusions. These distinct modes of behaviour reflected their ability or inability to perform rational work tasks. It appeared that there were two tendencies co-present in any one group: a capacity for real co-operative work, and a capacity to act out shared inner fantasies which shielded participants from the claims of reality.

The latter tendency Bion named 'Basic Assumption Behaviour'. The name is appropriate, designating a tacit assumption which lies behind a collective pattern of feeling and activity. The group behaves as if illusory notions were accurate perceptions of reality. These assumptions can be detected from the emotional state of the group and tend to take three forms. As these behaviours are never found in a pure form in society, description of them inevitably tends to caricature. But the descriptions are none the less useful for that (see Table 4.2 on page 40).

The Dependency Group behaves as if it were gathered to enjoy secure protection or direction by a great leader. People in this mode appear immature or inadequate, knowing nothing and wary of initiative. By contrast the leader they seek will be god-like in power and expertise. This idealized leader will care for and protect the others, making the complexities of life simple and absolving followers from the responsibility of action. No one can fill the expectations of this role though group members with ambition may be auditioned and rejected. Disappointment is endemic here and repeated attempts are made to urge a leader to become total carer by presenting a group member in extreme distress at the lack of security. This attempt at emotional blackmail is devised to force the leader to collude with the Basic Assumption Behaviour or be revealed as a cruel and unfeeling devil.

Such a group experiences greedy competition between members for leader attention. Desire for total dependence runs in tandem with a resentment of the infantilized condition. Mature behaviour is impossible because of the fantasies about the leader as a super being, who will control the irresponsibility of the group so that no one will get hurt.

In this mode the leader does not have to be a person. The writings of the long-dead

Table 4.2

			Groups		
Basic Assumptions Groups	Reason for group meeting	Distinctive behaviours	Defence against reality	Mythic features and roles	Specialized Work Group
Dependency	To be sustained by a leader	People behave as if they are immature and have nothing to offer.	Avoiding responsible action and seeing life as a whole	Dependants and Counter-dependants Leader is anti-hero, prophet or deity	Church
Fight/Flight	To fight or run away from something	People express paranoid feelings. There is talk of danger, enemies, 'them' 'us'. Actions are described in terms of courage and self-sacrifice.	Avoiding the enemy within	Struggle between good and evil – paradise lost Fight leader Flight leader	Army
Pairing	So that two people can pair off and produce the saving solution to the problem	People express hope of deliverance from present problems which deny and cover destructive feelings. Hatred and despair bubbles below the surface.	Avoidance of novelty or development by keeping a closed system	Messianic myths; the birth of the hero Mary and Joseph	Aristocracy

founder of an organization may be endowed with the ability to satisfy the dependency needs of his followers. They can be used to enable a group to develop a rigid mode of operation which provides security and a sense of group identity in the face of a hostile and fragmented world. Heretics who question the emerging orthodoxy are persecuted.

The Fight/Flight Group behaves as if the group had gathered together to preserve itself by attacking or running away from an imagined enemy. This is a risky group to be in for its weaker members, who may be wiped out in battle or abandoned in the retreat. As in war, casualties can be expected and heroic self-sacrifice is regarded as the noblest of behaviours. An appropriate leader for this group is someone with sufficient paranoia to locate an enemy when opposition is difficult to identify.

Bion comments that the leader of any assumption group is chosen

> not by virtue of his fanatical adherence to an idea, but is rather an individual whose personality renders him peculiarly susceptible to the obliteration of individuality by the Basic Assumption group's leadership requirements.[3]

This group rejects thought and analysis and is allergic to any self-reflection which could reveal internal conflict and divisions. All energies are directed outwards to flight or the defeat of some hated force of unmitigated evil. This group finds frustration difficult to tolerate and specializes in precipitous panic-driven actions which discharge painful feelings of rage.

The Pairing Group behaves as if the group was gathered to attend on the birth of a saviour. It relies on two members of the group pairing off to produce the messianic answer to everyone's problems. Though the pair need not be of different sexes, the basis of this illusion is reproduction and generativity. Interest in the activities of the creative pair is happily sustained and an atmosphere of hope pervades the group. All are living in the optimism of the birth of a leader in the form of a thought or structure which will answer present problems and usher in a new utopian age.

Hope fulfilled is hope extinguished. Any putative messiah will be rejected as inadequate. Consequently this group is ordained to bear no tangible results. All the positive talk about the future is to foster comfort and preserve an agreeable atmosphere in the present. This masks the fear of sterility in the face of new demands and worries about leaving the practices and attitudes of the past. Such a group has the rhetoric of futuring but it restricts the possibility of working with novel insights which members may contribute by encouraging collusion in an awe-struck silence before the creative pair.

Bion contrasted these Basic Assumption Behaviours with what he called the 'Work Group'. This mode of group behaviour is directed towards achieving the task of the group. Members of this group work co-operatively, using their personal insights and creativity to a common end. Ideas and conclusions are tested against reality and the group learns as it develops, acquiring expertise and self-understanding as time passes. The Basic Assumption Group exists without effort, seeking immediate gratification of its comfort needs. The Work Group, on the other hand, requires conscious application, recognition of difficulties and careful thought.

Bion did not denigrate Basic Assumption Behaviour in favour of the Work Group. Any group has to attend to its emotional dynamic if it is to achieve results. When in a work mode, Bion saw that group members harnessed and worked with one basic assumption which helped them to engage usefully with reality. Examples of this are the use schools and hospitals make of the Dependency assumption to help the young and the sick, and the Army's judicious use of Fight/Flight in wartime.

Basic Assumptions are not only a distracting interference with the work task, they can be the key to directing energy into productive activity.

> Work Groups can behave with sophistication and maturity, and we can use the Basic Assumptions to assist task performance; the emotions associated with one basic assumption are then used to control and suppress the emotions with others. Mature Work Groups expect their leaders to mobilize the appropriate assumption for task performance. If the appropriate assumption is Dependent, the leader has to be dependable but realistic; if Pairing, potent, but with due regard to the limitations of his potency; if Fight, constructively aggressive, brave but not foolhardy; if Flight, able to extricate the group from a difficult situation, but no coward, nor must he be able to solve all the group's problems in the process of extrication.[4]

Bion reinforces the importance of understanding Basic Assumption Behaviours by pointing out that people are predisposed to them and organizations are constructed to enact them. He refers to human beings' involuntary preference for a particular anxiety-reducing strategy as a 'valency'. These valencies predispose the individual to particular ways of handling the world and expressing themselves through certain careers or forms of life. The battle commander needs Fight/Flight tendencies, the educator mobilizes Dependency assumptions to teach the young, and Pairing is useful to family life and finds a sophisticated context in any one-to-one situation like counselling. Bion speculated that society sponsored sub-groups who processed Basic Assumptions on behalf of the culture as a whole. He identified these as the Church – concerned with absolute Dependency on God; the Army – reliant on the tactics of Fight or Flight; the Aristocracy – obsessed with lineage and good breeding demonstrating Pairing as a way of life.

Psychoanalysts have set much store in the myth of Oedipus, the man who set out to discover his parents and found himself guilty of patricide, regicide and incest. He is a supreme example of one who withdraws projections and faces the ambiguities of self. Like him, the mature Work Group can confront the paradox and ambivalence of reality. Oedipus answered the riddle of the Sphinx, recognizing man as the being who walks on four legs in the morning, two at noon and three in the evening. In doing this he showed his understanding of mutability of experience through time. Inspired by this, Margaret Rioch coined her own group-related riddle of the Sphinx.

> What is it that on Monday is wrangling, cruel and greedy; on Tuesday is indifferent and lazy; on Wednesday is effectively and intelligently collaborative? One could easily answer, 'That is man and it is also man in the group.'[5]

She shared Bion's confidence in the emergence of the Work Group, and believed that when a group faces reality it can work effectively and address its own fears. Those who have used these ideas to understand the workplace report similar experiences. However, they point out that the growing pains of working groups can be severe as many organizations have strong resistance to self-scrutiny.

SOCIAL DEFENCES AGAINST ANXIETY

All work involves making a difference: producing a car from raw materials and human skill; intervening medically so that the sick become healthy; in a school situation, moving pupils from unknowing into knowing. Organizations develop rational structures, technologies and operating methods to further their tasks. But whatever the context, participants worry that the anticipated transformations will fail to occur. This causes work practices and cultures to be significantly determined by the strategies workers devise to reduce their emotional stress.

> The needs of the members of the organisation to use it in the struggle against anxiety leads to the development of socially structured defence mechanisms which appear as elements in the structure, culture and mode of functioning of the organisation. A social system develops over time as a result of collusive interaction and agreement, often unconscious, between members of the organisation as to what form it will take. The socially structured defence mechanisms then tend to become an aspect of external reality with which old and new members of the institution must come to terms.[6]

If the work situation is perceived as threatening, much mental energy is used in defensive behaviour with correspondingly smaller amounts available for constructive activity towards the objectives of the enterprise. An example of this is the work of Isabel

Menzies, which analysed the way that social defences operative in a London hospital in 1959 affected nurse recruitment and patient care.

Contact with the sick is likely to cause anxiety. Despite the best care some patients do not recover and die. The professional life of the nurse is lived in the vortex of powerful feelings of pity and compassion towards the sick as well as resentment of those who do not get better. In addition to her own fears she has to cope with the guilt of relatives who have handed over 'their patient' to institutionalized care. The system developed techniques for mastering these anxieties which were then canonized as enduring examples of good nursing practice.

The nursing task was governed by shift systems and frequent movement of staff, which prevented the formation of nurse-patient relationships. There was a tendency to depersonalize individuals with staff rarely using patients' name. They referred instead to ailments, 'the ulcer in bed 3', or anatomy, 'the leg in bed 7'. Feelings evoked in distressing situations were quickly repressed by disciplinary exhortations to 'pull yourself together' or 'keep a stiff upper lip'. Emotional stress was said not to be a feature of the work, though senior staff suspected that this denial related to their inability to deal with the affective dimension of the work.

Anxiety levels were kept low by the ritualization of work. There was a standard procedure for every task, whether lifting a patient or distributing drugs. This reduced opportunity for disturbing initiatives or decision-making. In fact, there was a well-established procedure of delegating all decisions up the hierarchical ladder so that nurses were not responsible for patient care initiatives. During their training it became clear the nursing function provided little opportunity for personal development as it concentrated on the efficient implementation of pre-set activites. This went a long way in explaining the high drop-out rate among student nurses and accounted for low patient recovery rates in wards where there was low staff morale.

Students recruited on the basis of the hospital's 'nurses are born not made' philosophy were chosen because of their capacity for caring relationships with patients and their degree of personal maturity. Neither attribute was honoured in nursing practice, which offered little relational satisfaction or opportunity for initiative. The rigid working methods which had built up over the years did not serve new recruits, denying their ethic of personal care and requiring them to regress to a level of emotional immaturity and inability to cope commensurate with the organizational culture. Because the social defences of the hospital could not permit adaptation or development to suit the needs of newcomers the recruits frequently left.

This research has led to significant developments in nursing education and practice. It may also cause practitioners in other professions to think about the ways in which anxiety can inhibit beneficial changes to their own work activity.

SOCIAL DEFENCES AND CHANGE

The Menzies study helps to demonstrate that defences against anxiety play an important part in resistance to change. Institutional development requires an alteration in social defences which can reveal and intensify anxiety.

> The opposition and resistance to change can be understood by seeing it as the fear people have of relinquishing established social systems that have helped to defend them against

anxiety in the past. The old system will reflect the power and influence the previous generation had to shape the system to fit their own psychological needs. A change inevitably means
changes in power and influence, which will be reflected in new ways of operation and conse-
qently new social defence systems.[7]

The Basic Assumption Behaviours characterized earlier in this chapter provide access
to the impulses at the root of social defence systems. They support the strategies
employed to maintain comfortable understanding and activities among colleagues.
Three short descriptions of groups attempting to develop a multifaith approach to RE
in primary schools will illustrate this process.

Staff A cites history as a way of resisting change. Members express reservations about
their own professional competence, express respect for the LEA syllabus from the
1960s, recite the Bible or diocesan policy, and warn that the parents won't like it.
They may ask for 'expert' advice, which they discount on the grounds that the proposed approach would be too complicated for young children. The old ways are
seen as the *dependable* ways. The drift back into 'the way we were' becomes a
gallop and the group retreat into former practices. RE is confirmed as giving the
school a shared identity and there is no change.

Staff B is afraid that contentious issues may disrupt its fragile unity. They fear that
discussion about world religions would reveal irreconcilable differences amongst
staff. Scared of hostilities in the staffroom they *fight* off the initiatives, careful
not to engage in any professional talk which could cause dispute.

At a later date, the staff presents a cocktail of moral education, personal and
social education (PSE), multiculturalism and anti-racism as Religious Education.
Unable to correlate their legal obligations and their varied personal suspicions,
antagonisms and repudiations of faith traditions, such a staff can *retreat* from RE.
Afraid of what they see as proselytizing on the public purse, teachers caught in this
scenario run away.

In School C there is real excitement at the idea of expanding curricular offerings.
Everyone recognizes that it is a major task which will take some time. In the
interest of efficiency two creative people are delegated to work on it on behalf of
all. Everyone is confident that this *pair* will come up with the goods.

The larger staff group sustain great hope that the working duo will produce the
ultimate answer for all in the form of guidelines, lesson notes, or a training programme to deliver them from their worrying inactivity. In order to preserve this
optimism the working-party members huddle closer, working happily together
and fostering the great expectations of the rest. But the work is never completed.
Whatever they could offer would fall short of total deliverance. Nothing changes.
But this is a mere postponement of salvation day. The staff group confidently
expects that any day now . . .!

Scenarios such as these show that rational plans for change tend to founder because
they do not offer an exploratory dimension to the development process. Any effective
initiative needs an analysis of the shared concerns and unconscious collusions which
support customary activity. Unless those affected by developments have the time and
opportunity to investigate their psychological needs in relation to the new system,
attempts to modify institutional forms will incur suspicion, wrath and rejection.

LEARNING – A DIALOGUE OF THINKING AND FEELING

It appears that learning is a necessary prelude to change. This chapter has demonstrated the value of developing skills to understand the emotional dynamics of work. The spectrum of human awareness includes thought and feelings as mutually supportive sources of reliable knowledge about the world. Thought can free people from recurrent and futile rehearsals of repression and disaffection. Acknowledgement of the underlying sources of fear and anxiety is the first step in moving beyond them. Teachers take up their professional life cognitively disabled if they cannot use feelings about thoughts and thoughts about feelings to interpret the passions and pressures in primary school life.

In the last chapter, nine aspects of school life were identified as militating against curriculum and professional development. Four of them are sustained by emotional repression, which prevents staff from getting to grips with concerns that restrict school potential (see Table 4.3).

Table 4.3

Key factors in primary school life	Underlying issues	Consequences for difference
1. Concern with order	Fear of chaos	Differences are seen as disruptive. They disturb the status quo.
2. Maintenance of good relations	Fear of strong feelings and interpersonal conflict	Differences are not explored. When strong feelings are engaged the unity of the school is put at risk.
3. Vocationalism	Confusion of personal and professional commitments	Differences are subsumed by professional commonalities which are seen as more significant. Professional development is resisted if it conflicts with personal convictions.
4. The importance of right answers	Desire to minimize uncertainty	Difference and variety of cultural and religious practices are suppressed in the interest of a philosophy of 'one-right-wayism'.

The keys to releasing the energy needed for development may lie in

1. preparedness to use feelings as a significant resource for school development;
2. dismissing fantasies about schools as rational havens of order, unity, security and certainty;
3. recognizing that the value pluralism in society is inevitably reflected in the conflicting ethics and practices of people in schools;
4. developing a culture of discussion and exploration so that curriculum positions are the fruit of shared and informed understanding.

The psychoanalytic perspective provides one way in which staff groups can approach adult professional learning for curricular change. This type of development takes time and involves active reflection on a changing situation. The stories of primary school life offered in later chapters will show that a sophisticated use of the emotional energy of a staff group can enrich RE curriculum work.

NOTES AND REFERENCES

1.   *The Penguin Book of Women Poets* (1978) (London: Penguin), pp. 199–200.
2.   C. S. Hall and G. Lindzey (1968) 'The relevance of Freudian psychology and related view-points for social sciences' in E. Aronson and G. Lindzey (eds), *Handbook of Social Psychology*, Vol. I (Reading, MA: Addison-Wesley), p. 168.
3.   W. H. Bion (1968) *Experience in Groups* (London: Tavistock Publications), p. 177.
4.   A. K. Rice (1965) *Learning for Leadership* (London: Tavistock Publications), p. 27.
5.   M. J. Rioch (1970) 'The work of Wilfred Bion on groups'. *Psychiatry*, **33**, 56–65.
6.   I. E. P. Menzies (1970) *The Functioning of Social Systems as a Defence Against Anxiety* (London: Centre for Applied Research, Tavistock Institute), p. 10.
7.   R. de Board (1978) *The Psychoanalysis of Organizations* (London: Tavistock Publications), p. 143.

Chapter 5

The Environment and the Group

Ears in the turrets hear
Hands grumble on the door,
Eyes in the gables see
The fingers at the locks.
Shall I unbolt or stay
Alone till the day I die
Unseen by stranger-eyes
In this white house?
Hands, hold you poison or grapes?

Beyond this island bound
By a thin sea of flesh
And a bone coast,
The land lies out of sound
And the hills out of mind.
No birds or flying fish
Disturbs this island's rest.

Ears in this island hear
The wind pass like a fire,
Eyes in this island see
Slips anchor off the bay.
Shall I run to the ships
With the wind in my hair,
Or stay till the day I die
And welcome no sailor?
Ships, hold you poison or grapes?

Hands grumble on the door,
Ships anchor off the bay,
Rain beats the sand and slates.

> Shall I let in the stranger,
> Shall I welcome the sailor
> Or stay till the day I die?
>
> Hands of the stranger and holds of the ships,
> Hold you poison or grapes?
>
> *Dylan Thomas, 'Ears in the turrets hear'*[1]

The last chapter focused on the internal and fantasy life of working groups. It distinguished between the effective and ineffective group in terms of its connectedness to reality. This chapter explores external connections and pressures as a complementary way of understanding organizational life. If the emotional dynamic of working life needs illumination, then its political dimension also requires investigation.

SYSTEMS THEORY

Dylan Thomas's poem expresses the dilemma of those called upon to make connections between elements of their experience. Contact with the alien person or idea can prove damaging or life-giving. If the strange or the foreign is seen only as a threat it will be rejected out of hand. This ensures the survival of current operations but closes the door to development. Organizations are caught in a perpetual quandary: when to be open to outside influences; when to erect protective barriers to preserve things as they are.

Schools can experience the diversity of faiths and cultures in today's society in similarly threatening terms. Being open or closed to external influence is not simply a philosophical question. It functions urgently at a practical level, often having implications for curriculum, admission policy, school ethos and staff development.

'Openness' and 'closedness' are of vital concern in Systems theory. Strictly speaking, Systems theory is not an abstract theory at all. It is a biological and ecological perspective of the world which sees all systems – whether schools, factories or cinemas – in terms of living organisms which develop and thrive by responsive energy interchange with their environment. As a world-view, it is centred on the complex relations of the elements which make up a given system, be that a government department, school, or IBM. It proceeds by investigating the internal and external connections of an enterprise.

Systems theory developed as an aid to understanding and tracking the transfer and distribution of energy within a system. When human systems are subjected to a systemic analysis the flux and dynamic equilibrium which is the driving force of seemingly static entities is made apparent. It also reveals that the essential nature of the management within the system is to regulate exchanges with the environment across the boundaries of an organization.

School energy, resources, time and anxiety are inextricably connected with government, culture and the economy. Sound management of a school may involve internal restructuring to ensure survival in a turbulent era. This may be achieved by a school combining years 4 and 5 because of staff redundancy. If such changes in the pattern of work meet forms of internal resistance the smooth running of the institution may still be placed in jeopardy.

Table 5.1

Inputs from society	Educational process		Outputs to society
• Knowledge	*People*		People better fitted for
• Values	• Teachers	• Meals attendants	adult life in society
• Money	• Caretaker	• Crossing attendant	because of
• Curricular	• Special Needs Service	• Pupils	• Intellectual and
requirements	• Language Support staff		vocational skills
• Children	*Organization*		• Critical and reasoning
• Adults	• Classes	• Graded posts	capacities
	• Organizational hierarchy		• Spiritual awareness
	• Governors	• Inspectors	• Creativity and
	Technology		imagination
	• School buildings	• Books	• Communication skills
	• Curricula • Computers	• Buses	• Social responsibility
	Tasks		• Cultural understanding
	• Teach classes	• Issue reports and results	
	• Present budget	• Hire staff	
	• Produce plays	• Learn	

A management which ceases to spend energy on its external relations becomes a closed system, possessing dwindling resources for legitimate work. Such a situation calls to mind Bion's Basic Assumption groups, which are all closed systems.

On the other hand, there is no such thing as a totally open system. Such a thing would defy identification, merging with the environment because it lacked a boundary or distinctive task to separate itself from its surroundings. A school or any other system will be more or less open depending on its degree of productive interaction with factors in its context. In Table 5.1 the connectedness of the school to its environment is shown in terms of inputs and outputs.

Important systemic concepts are presented in Table 5.2, on page 50. These can provide a framework for developing management strategies responsive to a changing and plural world. In discussing the influences and pressures which environmental factors place upon the school, these concepts will be expanded.

KEEPING THE ENVIRONMENT IN MIND

Diagrams like Table 5.2 are seductive. They are logical and rational constructions and may misrepresent the reality they chart as equally logical and rational. The value of the exhibit resides in the way it indicates the aim, task, structures and boundaries of the school. It makes no assumption that these readily identifiable elements tell the whole organizational story. The Table does not include the way staff and pupils accept, ignore or redefine aims or working methods and use institutional structures for personal objectives.

Human beings always bring more to an enterprise than the activities or competencies they are asked to contribute. Adults and children carry across the school threshold their own agendas and beliefs, fears, hopes and concerns which are experienced more immediately than organizational goals. Participants 'survive' in the system by employing subtle means of accommodation to the discipline and requirements of the school. For the most part these are effective and there are no hiccups in the smooth

Table 5.2

Concept	Definition	Management consequences for schools as institutions	Curriculum consequences for teaching and learning
Holism	The relationship between parts of a system involving connectedness and integration	Should demonstrate coherence between espoused theory and theory in use brought about by collegial working styles	Contesting dualistic ways of interpreting the world
Cybernetics	The capacity to engage in intelligent self-regulation	Needs the insights of all personnel to steer a course towards the future	Commitment to fostering the pupil's capacity for learning to learn
Requisite variety	The internal regulatory mechanisms of a system as varied as the environment which is its context	Must have a realistic picture of the pluralism of its setting	Use of curriculum material from a variety of cultures, faiths and lifestyles
Equifinality	There is a variety of ways to achieve any given end; the structure at a given time does not determine the process	Should be flexible, able to change working structures and methods to achieve valued aims	Teaching and learning strategies which enable pupils to modify previously held patterns of knowledge and behaviour
Evolution	Capable of developing more complex forms of differentiation and integration depending on environmental demands	Should be able to develop structures to deal with particular interests or social conditions	Education regarded as a process which contributes to the self-development of pupils by giving experience of learning as adapting, interpreting and co-operating
Aim and primary task	The declared purpose of a system and the means by which that purpose will be achieved	Needs clearly stated purpose, e.g. Mission Statement	Creating a role for staff and pupils in relation to the aim and mission of the school
Boundary	The point of interface between a system and its environment	Depends on management as a life-giving boundary function	Openness and seeing learning as the response to the environment, which also creates the environment
Systems and sub-systems	A bounded set of purposeful activities and relations capable of interaction with its environment	Is most usefully pictured as a set of relations, rather than people or buildings	An educational approach centred upon making connections to previous experience and present events
Negentropy	The avoidance of dissipation of energy by being open to input and new sources of energy from the environment	Needs novelty and throughput of students/staff/ideas to retain health	Curriculum development so that educational process and content remains alive and relevant
Homeostasis and randomness	Maintaining a steady state of development responsive to unpredictable changes in the environment	Must retain a flexible responsive commitment to its purpose and working styles	Offering pupils a vision of an expanding world of opportunities for action

running of things. But when educational activities and philosophies conflict with the personal beliefs, attitudes and values of participants there can be severe disruption to work.

An examination of the way relations between personal history and institutional loyalties affect professional life throws light on the powerful forces which lead to internal rows and internal organizational disputes. This is explored in greater detail in the stories of school life in Chapter 8.

Shakespeare described people as players on the stage of life. When Jaques referred to men and women as playing many parts, he did not imply that they are perpetually engaged in acts of misrepresentation or dissimulation. He is saying that in differing circumstances we employ a variety of sincere and appropriate behaviours to achieve given ends. We engage productively with the world through a series of roles.

A role is an opportunity for action towards the achievement of a specific aim within a system (see Figure 1). The pupil role is to learn. The role of the teacher is to facilitate that learning through a range of socially mandated and sanctioned activities. No pupil or teacher is precisely like another. People wear their roles with a particular style, according to their distinctive personhood. They bring to them all their life's experience. Any role is infinitely capable of varied expression, depending upon the person who inhabits it.

However, a role is not an identity. The teacher role is just one among the many inhabited by the woman who is mother, wife, member of political and dramatic societies, consumer, daughter, etc. The behaviour and demeanour appropriate with class 4 would not help her to direct a play or campaign for elected office. Likewise, pupil behaviour will be inappropriate in a child's family context. Role behaviour will always be an inadequate expression of personal identity.

Pupils do not tend to see themselves totally in terms of the pupil role. The teacher, however, may be faced with a different situation. There is a tradition of teaching as a vocation, a professional expression of inborn personal predilections, affections, skills and values. This encourages teachers to put great personal investment in their professional activities and behaviour which can intrude on other areas of life. The teacher role and personal life can become mixed up. An example is the behaviour of the teacher who, at a social gathering, explains things with inappropriate simplicity; chastises youngsters on public transport for loud behaviour; or breaks up a street fight with the verbal formula used the day before on yard duty.

The consequent confusion between personhood and professional life presents problems in school life, too. If teacher behaviour, is inappropriately enacted in other spheres of life, there is also the tendency to seek curricular confirmation of personal values, attitudes and commitments. This can result in highly competitive or defensive staff meetings. The ability to work side by side in the educational process may mask conflicts of social and cultural values in a school. This enables staff members to assume a commonality of beliefs and attitudes as the foundation for an *esprit de corps* and positive school climate. The illusory notion is very fragile. Any curriculum development exercise or effort at shared policy-making has the potential to unleash a fight about deeply held principles acquired at the mother's knee. Staffrooms can become factional battlegrounds.

The teaching profession is made up of adults whose formative experiences reflect the variety of race, class, religious and political allegiances, lifestyles and ideologies which are found in society as a whole. This sedimented personal identity and history gives life and colour to the teacher role. It has the possibility of enriching staffroom debate but it makes consensus-building and decision-making a time-consuming and complex process. The school needs the energy and personal resources of staff and students if it is to develop. But it does not always have structures for processing the inevitable disagreements within an evolving educational culture.

> Value systems are highly personal and exceedingly complex and no two individuals share the same. Problems arise as individuals express personal values in behaviour with more than usual force or commitment. In organisations as a general rule, accommodation takes place with regard to normal behaviour but once behaviour changes it changes the 'profile' of personal values . . . Inherent in this process is a realignment of values – changes in what is or is not acceptable. The ways in which individuals permit conflicts to be resolved depend on personal value systems – an aspect of organisational behaviour usually neglected because too personal and therefore too risky.[2]

BOUNDARIES, PRESSURES AND POLITICS

The political features of intra-group conflict in the staffroom are power struggles, bargaining and the formation of coalitions to protect factional interests. Internal pressures such as these can threaten to destroy the organization from within. But, there are corresponding external constraints, interests and pressures which are a significant element in the development of policy and practice.

Schools are involved in a network of relations with organizations in their context, which exert varying degrees of authority, power and influence over their affairs. Proposals to alter the timing of the school day may, in the last resort, be defeated by the strict timetable of the local bus company. All schools have to maintain and manage their immediate connections with the DFE, government legislation, LEA requirements, parents, educational research, other schools, unions and educational suppliers. In some schools attachment to a particular religious denomination may determine admissions policy. In another, urban renewal plans may change a school's intake, making curriculum review essential.

If events in society can put pressure on schools to behave in particular ways, schools also influence the shape of society. School and society exist in a relationship of mutual causality. Developments in the educational system are a powerful political issue because they can be used to foster or undermine the aims and objectives of institutions and policy-makers in other spheres. Medical and legal professionals press for curriculum expansion to include health and social issues, such as AIDS and child abuse, which have been identified as problems in society. Diocesan authorities may question the wisdom of maintaining schools which do not deliver value for money in terms of supplying church members. Parents can require that the values of the home be supported in school. The Government can encourage governing bodies to have local employers as members, so that the needs of industry will be catered for within the school curriculum. These influences show educational practice to be the outcome of a very complex intergroup negotiation process. This can be threatening.

> . . . the setting up of any intergroup transactions has destructive characteristics since the relationship involved may destroy, or at least weaken, familiar boundaries. But any open

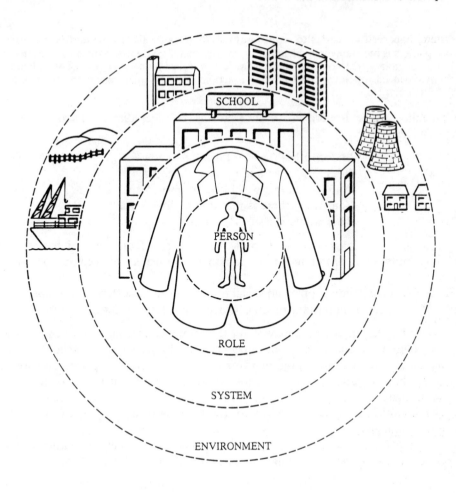

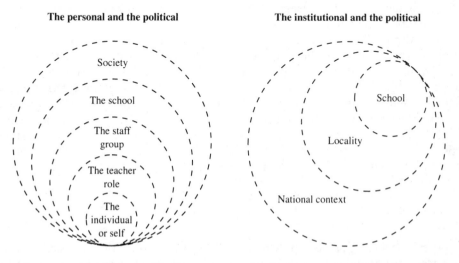

The personal and the political   **The institutional and the political**

Society

The school

The staff group

The teacher role

The individual or self

School

Locality

National context

Figure 1   *Person, role and system. The connections between the school and its environment.*

system, in order to live, has to engage in intergroup transactions. The members of any group are thus inevitably in a dilemma: on the one hand, safety lies in the preservation of its own boundary at all costs and the avoidance of transactions across it; on the other hand, survival depends upon the conduct of transactions with the environment and the risk of destruction.[3]

In 'Mending Wall', Robert Frost hints at the political dimensions of boundary management.

> 'Before I built a wall I'd ask to know
> What I was walling in or walling out,
> And to whom I was likely to give offense.
> Something there is that doesn't love a wall,
> That wants it down'.[4]

He recognizes the dangers of an approach to life based on imposed barriers and divisions, but the farmer in him is more convinced of the need to keep the cows out of the corn.

However, contact with people and social trends outside education can compel recognition of a variety of important realities which will affect the future of the school.

1. *Economic*: Unemployment may affect the family circumstances of pupils and the voluntary financing of some curricular offerings. Damage to school buildings may present an argument for opting out. Priorities placed on core curriculum subjects can leave a school without a competent RE curriculum co-ordinator.
2. *Demographic*: Property demolition or the building of new housing will affect pupil numbers.
3. *Political*: Publicity given to government emphasis on educational basics may lead parents to press for changes in curriculum and teaching methods.

Relations between schools and other institutions are difficult to talk about because 'schools' cannot have relationships. Only people can have relationships or take part in negotiations. Individuals or groups of individuals, in their educational roles, are involved with particular people who can represent or misinterpret the values, policies or intentions of the bodies they claim to serve. These relations take up a great deal of time and energy, and may be experienced as a coercive pressure to undertake a particular course of action which staff view with ambivalence. In many situations those involved may lose themselves in complex value debates about sexual behaviour, racial justice or religious identity in twentieth-century Britain. The final outcome has to be a practical curriculum proposal, relevant and accessible to a primary-age pupil. The distance between the passionate debates about society in the year 2000 and the nature of implementable class-room activity can bemuse and disappoint all involved.

BACK TO THE FUTURE

So far management has been presented as a function, rather than a specific job. It operates at the boundaries of the school, looking within to attend to the business of teaching and learning whilst at the same time looking outward to keep an eye on developments in the world. The task of management is to correlate the two, ensuring the survival and relevance of the school.

Systems thinking suggests cybernetics as a way of creating intelligent organizations which enjoy responsive relations with their environment. The word 'cybernetics' comes from the Greek word *kubernetes* which means 'steersman', one who succeeds in keeping a boat on course by a series of minor movements of the tiller. The vessel arrives at its destination by a series of corrections to an erroneous track. The steady course is maintained by a mechanism which automatically corrects itself, ensuring a reaction to any deviation outside specified limits. A thermostat also works on this principle.

In its simplest form cybernetics offers four principles to ensure a continuous process of information exchange between a system and its environment. A system must have the capacity:

1. to sense and monitor its environment;
2. to relate information received to the operating norm of the system;
3. to detect deviation from these norms;
4. to initiate corrective action when discrepancies are observed.

This is intelligent behaviour only to a point. The system is limited in its options by pre-existing operating norms. It functions logically only if environmental conditions are maintained. Should change occur, the information provided by negative feedback proves inadequate. Because it cannot question or alter its guiding norms, the system is committed to patterns of behaviour no longer relevant.

Applied to education, this is a recipe for a school becoming a prisoner of one successful period in its history. A nostalgic winning formula is repeated without regard for changed circumstances. Like the behaviour of the thermostat it assumes a recurring context. Cybernetic approaches adequate to an evolving context must include learning adaptive strategies so that staff can question the assumptions underpinning their existing practice. These two approaches have been described as single- and double-loop learning, and are explained in Figure 2.

Double-loop learning can be an uncomfortable experience. How do you examine the ground you are standing upon whilst still relying on it for support? What will happen if it should prove an inadequate base for the burdensome pressures of change? Simple single-loop learning is more appealing. Educational monitorial and assessment procedures introduced since 1988 follow this model. Teacher appraisal, pupil testing and proposed inspection procedures rely on assessing performance against pre-set objectives. These procedures are high on accountability and efficient task performance, but discourage institutional evolution which would require the acquisition of new behaviour and competencies.

MANIPULATION OR MANAGEMENT

There are many ways to discourage double-loop learning. In the day-to-day running of the school there is pressure for staff to be on top of their jobs; able to give a simple, rational account of what is going on, which shows that everything is under control. When the route to promotion depends on creating this good impression by giving support to existing practice, there is a disincentive for the individual to rock the boat

Single-loop learning

Double-loop learning

Step 1 = Examining and
    monitoring the environment.
Step 2 = Comparing this
    information with
    operating norms.
Step 2a = Questioning
    the relevance of
    operating norms.
Step 3 = Initiating
    appropriate action.

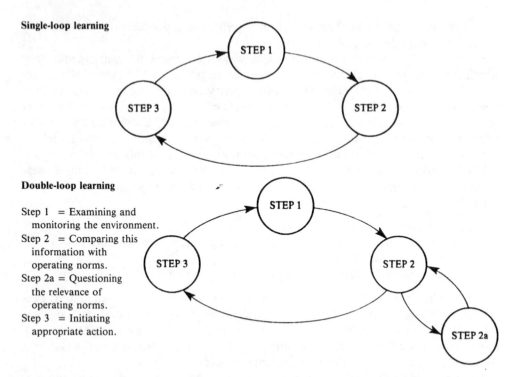

Figure 2   Single-loop learning depends on the capacity of a system to detect and correct error in relation to a given set of operating norms. Double-loop learning depends on the ability to take a second look at a situation by questioning the relevance of limited operating norms.

by questioning the basic educational and organizational beliefs underpinning current practice. Career interests are not served by acquiring the reputation of a trouble-maker.

However, the developmental needs of a school are not helped by the repression of insight and awareness which may hold the seeds of the future. Schools can choose not to respond to environmental events, offering arguments that counter-productive practices have to be maintained to satisfy an outside authority. The staff of an institution can claim participative working styles and openness by changing management vocabulary. The rhetoric of consultation, teamwork, negotiation and community links is a smoke-screen if actual practice is based on defensive structures closed to external challenge or internal thought.

School management from a systemic perspective would present a challenge to openness and flexibility at every level of organizational life. There are ten principles of systemic management.

Ten principles for systemic management

1. The school needs a clearly stated purpose, e.g. a Mission Statement.
2. The school depends on management as an energy-producing boundary function.
3. The school is most usefully pictured as a set of relations, rather than a group of people or a building.

4. The school needs novelty and throughput of students/staff/ideas to retain its health.
5. The school must retain a flexibly responsive commitment to its aims and working styles.
6. The school should demonstrate coherence between espoused theory and theory in use brought about by staff discussion.
7. The school needs the insights of all personnel to steer a course towards the future.
8. The school must have a realistic picture of the variety of its setting.
9. The school should be flexible, able to change working structures and methods to achieve valued aims.
10. The school should be able to develop structures to deal with particular interests and social conditions.

EVOLUTION AND THE ENVIRONMENT

Darwinian notions of natural selection have been applied to organizational ecology, suggesting that competition between species of organizations for limited resources is the determining factor in institutional survival. Since all systems and their sub-systems are involved in a process of mutual causality it may not be the 'survival of the fittest' which proves significant, so much as the 'survival of the fitting'. This sponsors the notion that systems can maintain themselves in existence by an ethic of collaboration rather than competition.

Despite the present climate of competition for pupils, some schools are organizing themselves into locally-based consortia for shared discussion and INSET provision. Such structures convert what were external relations of rivalry into internal relations of co-operation, which assist the recognition of common concerns and values amidst diversity. Such strategies will foster the survival of a variety of educational species.

This example of organizational ecology provides a model of the management of difference in the social context. But it implies criticism of that educational improvement tradition which identifies the 'right' or best way to do a thing and disseminates the strategy as generalized good practice. The initiative which enabled staff in one school to achieve a particular curriculum aim may not be replicable or even desirable in another context. Systemic thinking recognizes that there is more than one way to approach any issue. Organizations can move toward a chosen goal from different initial starting-points through a variety of means. A school may discover the best course of action only as staff understanding develops over time. Clear prescription of means and ends does not do justice to the creativity and flexibility of teachers or the complex and changing character of the environment in which they work.

LEARNING – A PROCESS OF RESTRUCTURING

When things are in a state of flux, learning is necessary to handle the changes. Development and variety are the hallmarks of organizations designed to cope. If a curriculum is to remain relevant, school aims, roles and structures will be in a continual process of review and redesign. This will be disconcerting, as people prefer to work with customary procedures and understandings even though these can fix relations between schools and their environments into counter-productive patterns. Teachers need to be able to reform and question inherited practices and alliances if they are to construct educational institutions able to meet the diverse requirements of government, parents and pupils.

Chapter 4 identified four fundamental emotional factors which counteracted the drive to diversity. Correspondingly, this chapter offers five aspects of school life affecting external relations which also work against serious curricular engagement with difference (Table 5.3).

Table 5.3

Key factors in primary school life	Underlying issues	Consequences for difference
1. Lack of clarity about aims	Cultural confusion	Differences are fudged. A discussion of aims would surface unexamined assumptions for investigation.
2. Tradition	Concern for the value of received wisdom and the status quo	Differences are repressed because they question inherited practices and attitudes.
3. Influence of external agencies	Concern that 'Education is too important to leave to teachers'	Differences arising from conflicts about power and authority are structured into the politics of the school.
4. Lack of cultural analysis	Reticence in making value judgements explicit	Differences of custom, race, morals and religion are seen as cultural curios.
5. Change overload	Stress produced by demands for rapid response	Differences are ignored in the face of 'greater priorities'.

Significant in making progress beyond these issues are

1.   preparedness to be open rather than insular;
2.   willingness to develop structures for curriculum talk and review;
3.   awareness of the variety of influences and pressures upon schools;
4.   readiness to identify, clarify and promote shared educational aims.

Looking at schools from a systemic perspective may be useful to those who wish to understand the complex interactions which affect the curriculum, teaching and learning strategies. Application is the best test of theory. The narratives of school life in Chapters 7, 8, and 9 will elaborate on Systems theory as a relevant resource for recognizing the complex influences on RE development in primary schools.

NOTES AND REFERENCES

1.   D. Thomas, *The Poems* (1971), edited by D. Jones (London: Dent), pp. 62–3.

2. H. Gray (1988) 'A perspective on organization theory', in A. Westoby (ed.), *Culture, Power and Educational Organizations* (Milton Keynes: Open University Press), pp. 152–3.
3. E. J. Miller and A. K. Rice (1975) 'Selections from systems of organization', in A. Coleman and W. Bexton (eds), *Group Relations Reader 1* (Washington, DC: A. K. Rice Institute), p. 61.
4. *The Complete Poems of Robert Frost* (1961) (London: Jonathan Cape), pp. 33–4.

Chapter 6

CREATE: RE Development in the Primary School

Either you will
go through this door
or you will not go through.

If you go through
there is always the risk
of remembering your name.

Things look at you doubly
and you must look back
and let them happen.

If you do not go through
it is possible
to live worthily

to maintain your attitudes
to hold your position
to die bravely

but much will blind you,
much will evade you,
at what cost who knows?

The door itself
makes no promises.
It is only a door.

Adrienne Rich, 'Prospective Immigrants Please Note'[1]

Using new resources, developing new perspectives, seeing the world differently is stimulating and dangerous. Invitations to novel ways of being or doing beckon us tantalizingly across the threshold of experience. Negotiating this route from the 'now' to the 'not yet' is to risk a change of view. Activities which have major ramifications are undertaken with caution, after much consideration. Only time will tell whether a change was valid, let alone safe. At the same time, people have a horror of missed opportunities. Adrienne Rich's poem carries a subtle warning that one person's gateway of opportunity is another's poisoned portal.

Taking part in any quest for understanding is rather like coming out of the woods and into the gingerbread house. Crossing the threshold will mean change, but one remains uncertain about the precise turn of events. This was evident in the experience of nine staff groups who took part in CREATE (Curriculum RE and Teacher Education), a project to understand the RE curriculum implications of pluralism and diversity.

RE: HISTORY AND MYSTERY

Questions about the purpose, nature and content of Religious Education function at the cutting-edge of the pluralism debate, taking seriously competing truth claims, beliefs and lifestyles. There is a strand in mainstream educational tradition which stresses the importance of teaching the child to question and think rather than passing on pre-packaged conclusions. This approach decries prejudice, requiring full informed and fair discussion of issues. A style of explicit RE has developed which presents pupils with the tenets, stories and festivals of major world faith traditions. This approach emphasizes the importance of accurate and ample factual information. It is a logical development, in line with the work of the cognitive theorists who thought that the source of any form of prejudice lay in ignorance, easily eliminated by having adequate and accurate information.

This information-based RE gained a wide advocacy

1. because it was seen as supportive of 'multiculturalism';
2. because of its emphasis on content;
3. because it is non-confessional.

A look at articles published in RE journals since 1980 would give the impression that this approach to RE is common practice in primary schools. The availability of multifaith teaching resources in bookshops and RE Centres appears to support this view.

However, this assumption was challenged in Bernadette O'Keefe's book *Faith, Culture and the Dual System*. It presented statistical and interview evidence from voluntary aided and county schools which showed that multifaith teaching, far from being the norm, was viewed with suspicion by significant numbers of teachers, parents and school governors. Her study describes the lack of INSET to update teachers' RE thinking and help them acquire knowledge of world faiths. She also reports a poor response to the Swann Report: 'The concept of multicultural education being of relevance to all children, including those attending 'all white' or 'all Christian' schools, has failed to impinge in practice for the majority of schools in our study'.[2]

Given the existing descriptive research, CREATE set out to identify and suggest a response to the attitudes which made RE development difficult in primary schools. Initial meetings with teachers revealed that RE in school was influenced by teachers' personal values and external pressures from church, parents and politicians. Successful project outcomes therefore depended upon working alongside staff groups as they attended to RE policy and practice, to specify and understand how these factors affected their feelings, expectations, deliberations, activities and curriculum practice.

A consultancy approach was adopted as the best method of putting CREATE's questions in touch with school experience. Group Relations, with its twin emphases on the psychodynamics of working groups and systemic relations within the environment, provided the methodological and analytic frameworks appropriate for this investigation.

The work was inspired by a vision of the rich RE curriculum possible if teachers had a positive view of pluriformity and human difference. Visions tend to be easier to state than enact. Transformation on this scale would not be achieved by issuing an A4 sheet of guidelines. Transformation is less about saving people from bad practice than the expansion of consciousness, described earlier in Nina Cassian's poem 'Ordeal'.

STRUCTURING THE WORK IN SCHOOLS

Since the exploration of difference was a key factor in the work, it was important to involve voluntary aided schools, Roman Catholic and Church of England, as well as those in the county maintained sector. CREATE initially sought participation from schools which reflected social, religious and ethnic diversity, as well as representing rural and urban experience. Trios of participating schools were located in areas centering on three large towns with racially diverse populations.

In 1987 the headteachers of 65 suitable primary schools were approached by CREATE with the offer of support for RE development. If the Head showed interest the idea was explored further with the staff as a whole, with a view to negotiating a regular time commitment for the group to meet over an eighteen-month to two-year period. Work began in nine schools in which staff agreed to take part.

Recruitment was affected by a dispute then taking place over teachers' contractual obligations to work on school premises for 1,265 hours. Many staff did not want to take on anything new at the time. Since CREATE offered an opportunity to engage in a shared activity nominated within headteachers' 'directed time', other groups were encouraged to undertake a basic commitment to one 90-minute session a month. As the work progressed school working parties grew up, and the consultant was increasingly involved in more aspects of school life. The monthly allocation of school time voluntarily given to this exercise increased greatly as time went on.

The trio cluster groups were relatively easy to set up in areas A and B. The school system in area C was experiencing unrest, caused by the policy of bussing ethnic minority children from the centre of town to county maintained schools in the suburbs. Heads of church schools felt themselves under pressure to justify their admission policies, and there was a general reticence to focus an educational spotlight on religion, which raised vexed issues of ethnicity and race relations. In the county maintained sector there was a reluctance to explore the adequacy of RE provision in such a turbulent context. It proved difficult to recruit to the programme in this area. After protracted discussions with many schools, CREATE decided to work with two church schools which did not have ethnic minority pupils, and a county maintained school which had recruited only Asian pupils. Work in these schools began in early 1988.

The nine schools had only one broad aim in common: to design and implement an RE curriculum which was

Table 6.1 *Schools in Area A*

	Number on roll	Location	Staff stability	Number of staff: October 1986	Selection reasons
County maintained	234	Inner-suburban, council housing estate	Stable	9 + 1p/t	Staff interest in RE development Headteacher's support for staff development through curriculum development Socio-economic environment of school
Church of England	89	Rural	Stable and hoping to add a deputy	3 + 1p/t	Small size Admissions policy Strong church connections
Roman Catholic	157	Town centre	Stable	8	High proportion (70 per cent) of ethnic minority pupils Staff interest in RE development Headteacher interest in exploring the 'anomalous look' of school

Table 6.2 *Schools in Area B*

	Number on roll	Location	Staff stability	Number of staff: October 1986	Selection reasons
County maintained	790	Town centre	Stable	28	Size of the school High turnovers of pupil population Interest in Re curriculum development
Church of England	126	Large village in rural setting	Stable	6	Staff interest in RE development Rural location Headteacher interested in whole-staff development exercise
Roman Catholic	430	Inner-suburban	Stable	13	Staff interest in RE development Headteacher interest in whole-school development through a common staff development programme

1. adequate to the needs of the pupils;
2. appropriate to the setting of the school;
3. implementable by the staff.

All of the staff recognized this as a professional development exercise, which involved learning from one's own experience of working in groups. In retrospect, only eight of the nine headteachers recognized that progress towards the stated aims would affect the institutional culture and the authority and decision-making structures in the school.

Three months into the work, each school contracted for the RE development work to have a particular focus, e.g. assemblies, RE topic work, or narrative in RE. A sub-

Table 6.3   *Schools in Area C*

	Number on roll	Location	Staff stability	Number of staff: October 1986	Selection reasons
County maintained	60	Town centre	New school	Head + 2	100 per cent ethnic minority pupil population Headteacher support for an ongoing staff development exercise Only county maintained school prepared to spend time in this way
Church of England	185	Inner-suburban	Stable	8	Staff concern over admission policy Staff interest in RE development Headteacher support for whole-school professional development initiative
Roman Catholic	123	Outer-suburban	Stable	4	Diocesan admissions policy Headteacher support for staff development through curriculum development The only RC school in area to register interest

sequent renegotiation and redefinition of these nominated areas was a crucial stage of the work.

The work began with a series of monthly post-school meetings of 90 minutes, attended in eight cases by the whole staff group and in the ninth school by a delegated working party of seven. The emphasis was on collegial work to bring about curriculum development.

Significant findings emerged from the behaviour of the groups themselves. The staffs learned by making connections between their behaviour and experience – their intentions, feelings, beliefs, impressions, uncertainties, anxieties, and external pressures. The teachers monitored their own experiences and, in deciding how and when to discuss that experience, they furthered the learning and development work of the group. As the study developed, staff groups were able to address gaps in their own knowledge and identify resource needs. Six of the participant staff groups identified an increased capacity to collaborate in a diverse working team as the most significant outcome of the programme. This grew out of their ability to harness their rich and varied resources in the interests of their pupils, rather than going for the lowest common denominator of staff agreement.

The nine staffs could not meet their varied needs in one common RE programme because their schools were different in terms of foundation, socio-economic setting, ethnicity of intake, curricular structuring of RE, and the faith tradition of the pupils and teachers. Six of the eight groups, which worked with CREATE for two years, articulated and wrote RE curriculum policies, with five also designing syllabus material to facilitate their implementation.

Information about world faiths proved useful; testing new teaching strategies was refreshing; but development and new insights emerged from the shared struggle with their own differences of faith, values, teaching styles and responses to the pluralist society. Now differences were not

1. factors to be suppressed to preserve the peace or the status quo;
2. exotic practices in the worship, beliefs and diet of other people.

Differences were now

1. a natural dynamic of group life to be explored so that the school could renew itself;
2. the vital lived commitments and values of people which shape the world.

Eight of the original nine groups reported an increased understanding of the forces at work in their own context which contributed to making RE a contentious area. One school discontinued the development work after three meetings, uncomfortable with the exploratory style of the work. The CREATE consultancy surfaced competing values and interests, and examined how changing circumstances influenced curricular decisions made by staff groups working together. In this it did not set out to recommend or undermine any given outcome but to understand the events, issues and anxieties at work in nine such situations.

These instances remain discrete examples of collegial RE development in the late 1980s, but they highlight relational dynamics which affect both RE development work and work in other curriculum areas.

CONSULTANCY: AN AID TO SELF-REFLECTION

From the outset the work in school was framed and described to potential participant staffs in consultancy terms, i.e. working with group process, monitoring behaviour as it happens, exploring connections between the school and its context. The challenging implications of this method of working only became clear to all participants as the exercise developed.

Despite the early talk about the importance of attending to the feelings, attitudes and thoughts of teachers evoked by RE, participants tended to see the purpose of the exercise as the trouble-free implementation of new syllabus provision. Even though initial contact with schools brought to the surface the need to examine conflicts over current practice, the groups tended to block consultancy in this area, reinterpreting the consultant role as that of expert in world faiths or validator of present practice. The tendency was to view 'our consultant' as someone whose job it was to ensure happiness for all. Compliance with this expectation would have been to collude with the Basic Assumption Behaviour of the staff groups.

The consultant had to be aware of the defences against anxiety which diverted the staff group from real work. This led to tension in all of the groups, and one school parted company with CREATE at this point. Others came to recognize that rejection of the consultant's interpretations was a strategy to reduce the challenging possibilities of the undertaking. At this point many renegotiated the original working contract made with the consultant, which they now acknowledged served only to limit the scope of the exercise and protect entrenched attitudes. New work arrangements were more fluid and radical in that they did not exclude contentious areas from investigation.

There was growing recognition that curriculum development had to be preceded by the personal and professional development of teachers. The ability to explore personal attitudes to difference and religious pluralism was central to RE development. From this time onwards, there was an understanding that the consultancy was not merely about syllabus change based on expert direction, but was concerned with the development of the thinking and attitudes of the teachers themselves. This was bound to have its traumatic and confrontational moments. The consultant needed to exercise discretion in attending to and interpreting the Basic Assumption states of the groups. The teachers were personally and professionally vulnerable, looking to the consultant to contain their anxieties and help their transformation into a group capable of constructive work.

CHANGE AND TRANSFORMATION

Transformation is not change writ large. The difference between these two concepts is one of kind rather than degree. Change leads to new organizational activities and procedures, whereas transformation leads to the development of insight and self-understanding.

The making of change is an essentially reactive phenomenon. It assumes a scenario where alteration in contextual conditions demands an organizational response. People may resist, attempting to preserve the system as it is by sheer inertia. But they eventually comply, to some extent, by arranging things so that few valued attitudes and practices are sacrificed whilst maximum gains in the new regime are secured. From the outset, change initiatives are governed by predetermined and explicit objectives which are achieved through the exercise of power. In Bion's terms, the Basic Assumption, Fight, is mobilized so that people can come to terms with the threatening new developments with a well-rehearsed battle plan.

The territory of transformation is pervaded by a general sense within a person or group that things are no longer what they once were. There is an awareness that established personal or organizational identities are under threat from disruptive feelings within the individual or institution. The cause of the disquiet is difficult to locate and presents itself as an unknown irritant. This mysterious entity, its meaning and implications, can only be discovered given time and structure to attend to the behaviour of people stressed by the process of emergence and becoming. This requires patience.

The temptation is to fly from the challenge of transformation, with its imperative of self-development, into a flurry of change. This Flight ensures the replacement of discomforting unease with a series of structured activities capable of 'common sense' evaluation. This is an altogether less demanding undertaking. Compared with transformation, change promises certainty and security. The nominated aims and schedules of a future-oriented change process do not raise the anxieties triggered by the quest for latent meaning which awaits disclosure in a frustrating present.

THE FLIGHT TO CHANGE

The initial intention of the consultancy, 'exploring teachers' own religious and religious educational presuppositions and the ways they impact on school policy', was lost sight of by staff members as soon as work began. The immediate pressure was to achieve success. The working aims expressed in the contracts formulated a few weeks earlier became understood in terms of the achievement of specified changes.

There was widespread uncertainty as to the curriculum place, purpose and content of RE, with all the attendant concern for matching personal and professional commitments with alleged 'good practice'. Then it was as if this cloud of unknowing lifted. Not only did each staff suddenly appear to know precisely what the root of their RE difficulty was, but they also knew precisely the strategy needed to relieve it. In this mode the consultant was expected to be the expert who would supply relevant training techniques, resources and set deadlines to ensure achievement of stated goals. It would have appeared to an outsider, arriving when participants were in this phase, that the exercise was about efficiency in collegial approaches to curriculum innovation.

In 1987/88 there were particular encouragements to this flight to change:

1.   the pressure for headteacher 'directed time' to be used to demonstrably good effect;
2.   the proliferation of articles and INSET approaches which emphasized the effective implementation of change;
3.   political debate about the Education Reform Act alerting teachers to the extent of coming changes in the primary curriculum.

The consultant, too, felt a pull to join in the gadarene rush to change. The struggle to represent the need for patience was an important feature of project experience. It was tempting to satisfy participants' anxiety with a demonstration of conceptual and analytical competence, and to soothe them into dependant confidence. But the offer of easy solutions to problems, would have robbed others of their space to learn. Group Relations consultancy is valuable only if the consultant can hold the doubts and suspicions of others till a pattern for exploration emerges.

The emergence of this distinction between change and transformation was to prove fruitful in the work of CREATE.

1.   It explained the general 'flight to change' in the participating staff groups.
2.   It accounted for the consequent recovery of nerve and reinstatement of the Group Relations process as the only way to achieve genuine understanding of the school dynamics affecting RE attitudes and policy.
3.   It illuminated the uncomfortable connections between professional and personal development, especially in areas concerned with beliefs and values.

Change and transformation offer alternate ways of processing one's experience of difference. Preference for ordered and predictive procedures lends support to change rather than transformation. This reinforces the culture of control and closed questions, discussed in the first part of this book.

THINKING FOR CHANGE AND TRANSFORMATION

Change is organized in accordance with a widely accepted understanding of thinking and thought. 'Thinking for change' assumes that thoughts are the conceptual products of an intellectual process called 'thinking', undertaken by an individual thinker. Thoughts are either true or false. They are the property of the thinker who can elaborate, manipulate or teach them to others. These thoughts are considered to be so valuable that institutions are set up to preserve and disseminate them to others. In the educational world these can take the form of curriculum action plans, INSET initiatives or national programmes.

Unfortunately, this kind of thinking produces thoughts and assigns them value long after their shelf-life has expired. At the point when they become dangerously counter-productive, the sponsoring organization has often developed its own momentum and will to survive. Despite these limitations 'thinking for change' provides the engine to many an educational venture. It is attractive because this common-sense approach is seen to provide ready measures of the changes effected. It is less useful in helping to answer the vexed question of whether the particular changes advocated respond to the real or the fantasized situation.

The thinking underpinning attempts at transformation may prove more useful in this regard. In 'thinking for transformation' thoughts discover the thinker and thinking is the capacity for the effective communication of thoughts. The role of thinkers is to make themselves available to be discovered by thought. To be available for thought is to stand outside of remembered interpretative frameworks and hopes for the future, remaining open to surprise in the present. John Keats saw this as a hallmark of creativity and called it Negative Capability:

> Negative Capability, that is when a man is capable of being in uncertainties, mysteries, doubts, without any irritable reaching after fact – to let the mind be a thoroughfare for all thoughts, not a select party.[3]

Leonard Bernstein, the composer, saw this disordered state as the seed-bed of creative intuition.

> I sit for long nights all by myself and don't have a thought in my head. I'm dry. I'm blocked, or so it seems. I sit at the piano and just improvise . . . And then suddenly, I find a note that hits, that suggests something else . . . The mind where all this creativity takes place, is an immensely complicated circuitry of electronic threads . . . But every once in a while there is something like a short circuit; two of them will cross, touch and set off something called an idea.[4]

Thoughts so discovered are used immediately and do not have any enduring worth. They are stepping-stones to further development. No institution can be set up to preserve the 'great insights' because there are likely to be a continuing series of breakthrough perceptions which breed their own redundancy. People and organizations shaped by this kind of thinking are at risk of continual revolution. The skill of 'thinking for transformation' can only be demonstrated by an increased capacity to find and name thoughts which disclose the complex reality of the situation-in-mind.

'Thinking for transformation' can be a useful educational tool because of its capacity to identify the significant factors affecting practice in school. In Group Relations terms it represents the suspicion of Basic Assumption Behaviour and flight into change and activity. It also rescues consideration of emotional experience from the realm of private, personal or involuntary feeling, and recognizes that primary experience is a source of knowledge about the objective world.

EMOTIONAL EXPERIENCE AND CREATE

This description of 'thinking for transformation' emphasizes the importance of emotional experience. This is commonly understood as the locus of private feelings, passions and mental sensations stimulated by memory or anticipation. These feelings are learnt, definite and nameable, and their expression is part of day-to-day social interaction.

Primary emotional experience, on the other hand, provides the driving force of transformation and was the key to the work of CREATE. It is antecedent to communication through language. These undifferentiated states which precede conceptual formation are contagious and spread from one person to another by projective identification, producing a shadowy sense of a threatening condition yet to be realized. The lines of this poem sum up the frightening anticipation.

> Like one that on a lonesome road
> Doth walk in fear and dread,
> And having once turn'd round, walks on,
> And turns no more his head;
> Because he knows a frightful fiend
> Doth close behind him tread.

Samuel Taylor Coleridge, The Rime of the Ancient Mariner[5]

The threatening emotional state may presage a novel connection with reality or some abberant fantasy.

It was the capacity to stay with the hard task of discerning reality which opened staff groups to transformation. This distinguishes learning from experience from learning by experience, which relies on diagnosis of a catalogue of costly disasters.

The CREATE consultancy identified the boundaries of emotional experience to be explored in each school as coextensive with the 'school-in-the-mind' of participant staff members. This recognised that emotional experience is a systemic property being made by and affecting the staff as a group. Investigation of this experience was not a matter of individual psychoanalysis but depended on an appreciation of the relatedness of the group and how they were connected to the experience of wider society.

CREATE discovered that the school-in-the-mind was a vast entity. It encompassed history, social issues, concern with freedom and the limits of the authority of the various partners in education. Significant issues in the consultancy were:

1. teachers' ambivalence about their personal beliefs and religious histories;
2. religious and racial intolerance in schools and society;
3. LEA and denominational RE policy at diocesan, regional and national level;
4. fears and sensitivities aroused by the Salman Rushdie affair;
5. identifiable staff resistance to the advocacy of ideologies in school;
6. the use of RE for behaviour modification in pupils;
7. the exclusion of RE from the core curriculum in England;
8. pressures for voluntary aided Muslim schools.

As staff groups assembled the factors affecting their practice, they called to mind the children observed by the farmer in Patrick Kavanagh's poem 'The Great Hunger',[6] who

. . . sat on the railway slope and watched the children of the place
Picking up a primrose here and a daisy there –
They were picking up life's truth singly. But he dreamt of the Absolute envased
    bouquet –
All or nothing. And it was nothing. . . .

These lines catch the peculiar excitement of separate discoveries and the frustrated desire for the complete revelation and total resolution of all and everything.

This yearning for totality, the big understanding, provided an unexpected aspect to CREATE work. Despite the way the RE exercise had been framed, staffs used it as a vehicle for processing a variety of unanticipated issues which were central to the life of their particular school, e.g. racial prejudice, school survival, staff solidarity.

It may be that RE has the capacity to reach the parts that other subjects cannot reach, and move basic matters of school values, mission and culture to the top of the agenda. The process consultancy undoubtedly worked to draw out aspects of institutional life which had never found a safe arena of exploration.

The following three chapters offer a series of accounts and reflections on CREATE work in schools. They spell out what is involved in picking up school 'life's truth singly', and point beyond themselves to the importance of Group Relations working methods as a tool for curriculum innovation.

NOTES AND REFERENCES

1. *Poems Selected and New 1950–1974* (1975) (New York: W. W. Norton), pp. 65–6.
2. B. O'Keefe (1987) *Faith, Culture and the Dual System* (Brighton: Falmer Press), p. 148.
3. *Letters of John Keats*, edited by R. Gittings (1987) (Oxford: Oxford University Press), p. 43.
4. L. Bernstein quoted in M. Fox (1979) *A Spirituality Named Compassion* (Minneapolis: Winston Press), p. 129.
5. *The Poetical Works of Samuel Taylor Coleridge* (1893), edited by J. D. Campbell (London: Macmillan), p. 106.
6. *Collected Poems* (1972) (London: Martin Brian & O'Keefe), p. 41.

Part Three

Case Studies

The chapters in Part Three follow the course of eight staff groups as they developed the RE curriculum over a two-year period. They show how history, personal conviction, political commitment and environmental factors influence teachers' curriculum debate and practice. In Chapter 9, a narrative model of staff development is proposed.

Chapter 7

Passion and Pluralism

Whatever I find if I search will be wrong.
I must wait: sternest trial of all, to contain myself,
Sit passive, receptive, and patient, empty
Of every demand and desire, until
That other, that being I never would have found
Though I spent my whole life in the quest, will step
Clear of the shadows, approach life a wild, awkward child.

And this will be the longest task: to attend,
To open myself. To still my energy
Is harder than to use it in any cause.
Yet surely she will only be revealed
By pushing against the grain of my ardent nature
That always yearns for choice. I feel it painful
And strong as a birth in which there is no pause.

I must hold myself back from every lure of action . . .
And then as in dreams, . . . I begin
To understand, in fragments, the message she waited
So long to deliver.

Ruth Fainlight, 'The Other'[1]

These verses are forged out of the strong feelings which attend the birth of a child, idea, poem or institution. The promise of the new can generate the energies necessary for its realization through active engagement. But the poem suggests that the vital elements in giving birth are contemplative attention, waiting and patience. Its author sees birth as the fruit of revelation rather than labour. This provides the perfect analogy for the painful process 'thoughts in search of a thinker', which cuts across the ethic of human striving and requires passivity.

The work ethic persuades people that correct procedures and effort make all things possible. This fails to recognize that much human effort is squandered on the heartfelt quest for a truth which eventually unfolds itself, or the search for the key to a door which was never locked. All of this is executed in the white heat of passion for some new creation. People pursue this grail, debilitated as much by fervour as by the effort to control it.

Religious tradition offers many stories of miraculous births, divine interventions and redemptions. Perhaps it's an occupational hazard that participants in RE development misconstrue their task as Messiah-making or the manufacture of their own salvation. Carrying such unrealistic aspirations, these exercises are inevitably volatile affairs.

The case studies presented in this chapter centre on the feelings and emotional experience of three staff groups involved in RE development work. They focus on the way in which personal history, commitment, memory, and expectations impact on professional life. They are stories of the struggle against overwhelming anxiety and the effort to stay in touch with reality. The three cases show how pupil experience in the class-room can be determined, interpreted and edited so that staffroom unrest can be kept within teacher-manageable limits.

GEORGE STREET COUNTY PRIMARY SCHOOL

Developing a different staff working style

George Street Primary was built in the 1960s. A light and airy school set in playing fields, it is built on a council housing estate in the suburbs of a large town with a significant ethnic minority population. The majority of the pupils come from the immediate area. Many of their families are in receipt of Social Security benefits and 25 per cent of the pupils receive free school meals. There are few ethnic minority pupils as the town's Asian population lives in the town centre. There are 234 pupils and nine staff.

The headteacher had been pursuing policies to raise academic standards in the school. He was also taking a course in educational management and questioning his own, self-identified, autocratic leadership style. Impressed by his reading about collegial management practices, he was keen to undertake a long-term staff development exercise which would involve collaborative working. At this juncture he was approached to join the CREATE venture.

The staff were interested in having a focus for the recently introduced 'directed time', and agreed that RE, currently a dimension of topic work, was ready for a review. People readily acknowledged their varying discomforts in relation to RE.

'I never feel at ease with RE. I'm not really sure that it should be on the timetable. I'm not sure where education ends and brainwashing begins. But may be that's just me and my atheismhumanism.'

(Fieldnote)

'This is Britain and I think that we all would agree that it's important for children to understand the Christian tradition before they hear about other religions. Some of the children here have never been in a church even though there's one 200 yards down the road.'

(Fieldnote)

'It's important for people to think about religion and have values for life. But I'm not confident about my teaching. I don't know much about the religions of the world. But I think that everyone has to be tolerant.'

(Fieldnote)

Given the variety of assumptions and attitudes towards RE expressed in the opening discussions it was not surprising that the group proved reluctant to address religion directly. They identified a clear use for RE as a tool for behaviour modification in pupils. They were keen to develop this into a programme focusing on human relationships in groups. They saw this tying in with a current school initiative to develop clear disciplinary guidelines within the school's pastoral policy. This approach would avoid any embarrassing exploration of the different values and attitudes present in the staff and unite them in devising syllabuses and lesson plans designed to produce polite, well-behaved pupils who would not fight amongst themselves. Work on a multifaith approach to RE was ruled out on the grounds that it was irrelevant to the majority white pupils, whose parents would find it problematic.

The proposed work echoed their own recently negotiated position in the RE review, not to risk disagreement among themselves. But at another level the original decision to focus on an exploration of relationships in groups indicated a hope that the school and those working in it would be empowered if the energies of everyone were constructively harnessed. It was certainly the Head's ambition that process consultancy would have an effect beyond the RE curriculum and inaugurate a more collaborative approach to school management.

The agenda the staff initially chose to pursue could be seen in Bion's terms as a Flight from religious conflict. Members of staff valued the support and co-operation of colleagues and were worried that disagreement over faith and religious truths could damage staff solidarity.

'We all have personal and individual beliefs and I've been criticized in the past for expressing my faith position in school. In fact, I'm not allowed to teach RE because I'm not neutral enough. I'm not sure I want to risk it again here.'

(Fieldnote)

The decision to look at human relationships seemed to promise unity, as everyone was in favour of good relationships. The problem for the staff in working at their task was that there was a variety of opinions as to which values and behaviour made for good relationships. There was a reluctance to spoil 'a pleasant enough' working environment by reflecting upon the principles and values which underpinned useful behaviour in groups. The real flight was not from religion but from an acknowledgement of diversity within the staff group.

God was invoked by one person as the supreme judge of values.

'Before we talk about values at all, I think we've got to establish the authority of God.'

(Fieldnote)

Most staff were unhappy with a theological scaffolding for their anthropology, but all behaved as if there were some available arbiter to authoritatively define the values to be held by all, lived by all and taught to all. This ultimate reference could be relied upon to tidy up inconvenient differences. This group fantasy indicates the presence of the

Basic Assumption, Dependency. The Dependency was reflected in expectations that the consultant, headteacher or somebody would take charge, do all the work and prescribe norms for human relations which the others would accept.

> Deliver the goods!
> Say something to inspire us!
> Tell us of our own greatness!
> Divine our secret desires!
> Show us the way out
> Make yourself useful!
> Deliver the goods!
>
> Stand alongside us, so that
> You tower over us
> Show us that you are one of us.
> We'll make you our hero. . . .
>
> Know that our great showmen
> Are those who show what we want to have shown.
> Dominate by serving us!
> Endure by naming direction for us
> Play our game . . .
> Deliver the goods!
>
> *Bertold Brecht, 'Deliver the Goods'*[2]

As the group proceeded with attempts to coerce the consultant to do the work for them, some members recognized a typical staff meeting's pattern.

> 'This reminds me of a lot of our staff meetings. Here we are trying to get the outside expert to come up with the answers. Normally we are sitting waiting for the Head to give us the last word. That's very convenient. We don't have to make any effort and can criticize if anything goes wrong.'
>
> *(Fieldnote)*

Professional behaviour in the staff group had become the real focus of attention. There was a developing understanding that the key to their class-room programmes lay in sorting out their own experience in the staffroom, so that they would take more responsibility in curriculum management. They were making a movement from a belief in applied educational technologies towards a reflective engagement with their own working practices.

Freed from the obligation to have all the right answers, the staff were honest about their own fears and insecurities about teaching in a changing social, moral and cultural climate. Elements in the life of the community which individuals identified as worrying trends – unemployment, one-parent families, changing sexual mores, religious diversity, racial discrimination, increasing secularism – were factors in their own lives. Their quest for normative culture and values robbed the staff of their own experience and would not help pupils to deal with the reality of twentieth-century Britain.

The teachers in George Street Primary set about a radical review of their RE scheme with the intention of representing a plurality of lifestyles, beliefs and values. They did not want to pass on to the pupils the fear of differences which had been so powerful in the staff culture. The response of pupils to visits to churches, mosques and temples, and the general parental support those received, confirmed the staff in the usefulness of this approach to RE.

THE USES OF CONSULTANCY

In George Street, as in the other schools, participants claimed that the uses and resources of consultancy were difficult to recognize and appropriate. To acknowledge that there was benefit in facilitation of a professional meeting was felt to imply criticism of teachers' skills in curriculum development and the ways that they had worked in the past. Ken Rice says that the job of process consultant is

> to draw attention to group behaviour and not the individual behaviour; to point out how the group uses individuals to express its own emotions, how it exploits some members so that others can absolve themselves from the responsibility of such expression.[3]

Considered abstractly these are informative and potentially fruitful behaviours. But they are capable of an aggressive interpretation by participants, invited by a consultant to attend to their own manipulations and avoidances. Often a consultant's comment on the group's behaviour was ignored or labelled a distraction.

> 'Every time we seem to be getting somewhere, the consultant's helpful remarks dump us back in the swamp. I think it's done deliberately so that we don't get anywhere and look a right bunch of lemons.'
>
> *(Fieldnote)*

There was an expectation that the consultant was the expert, whose real job was to impose 'good practice' on the school. This suspicion was born out of staff experience of 'cascade' approaches to INSET which gathered groups together 'to facilitate a smooth and uncritical adoption of preferred forms of action introduced and imposed by experts from elsewhere, in which teachers become technicians rather than professionals exercising discretionary judgement'.[4] So the preferred image of the consultant was that of teacher or super-teacher; the one with all the answers; the total saviour on whom everyone could depend for instant solutions to every circumstance.

> 'Why don't you just tell us what to do and then we'll get on with it.'
>
> *(Fieldnote)*

When the consultant failed to take up this role, consultancy was rejected as having nothing to offer. Leadership was then given to someone who kept others happy temporarily by postponing decisions, repressing differences and denying the need for any development.

At these times the consultant was used as a receptacle for group despair and negativity. In dismissing the consultancy the group appeared to be projecting onto it all of its own guilt, incapacity and inaction. The consultant was now cast in the role of a scapegoat or Sin Eater.

> In Wales . . . mostly in rural areas, there was a personage known as the Sin Eater. When someone was dying the Sin Eater would be sent for. The people of the house would prepare a meal and place it on the coffin . . . The Sin Eater would devour

this meal . . . It was believed that all the sins of the dying person accumulated during his lifetime would be removed from him and transmitted to the Sin Eater. The Sin Eater thus became absolutely bloated with other people's sins. She'd accumulate such a heavy load of them that nobody wanted to have anything to do with her; a kind of syphilitic of the soul, you might say. They'd even avoid speaking to her, except when it was time to summon her to another meal.[5]

This excerpt from Margaret Atwood's story is a useful analogy of some crucial aspects of the consultant role. But the consultant functions to contain anxiety, aggression and despair, not to carry these elements into exile. This suggests the possibility that these feelings need not totally overwhelm the group. In addition, the process consultant acts as a thinker, drawing together the confused elements of others' experience into meaningful patterns.

In George Street, as in many other schools, it was only well into the work that the staff could fully recognize the consultant's confrontation of the group as an aid to productive work rather than a slap across the wrist.

> 'You are very crafty. I've been watching you. You gave our behaviour back to us. You are like a mirror in which we can see ourselves. I don't always like what you make me see, but some of it is uncomfortably right.'
>
> *(Fieldnote)*

When the consultant's example of the containment of pain and its consequent transformation through thought was adopted by staff members, the group could discover its own 'mind' and begin to work.

These reflections on the George Street story tend to suggest that consultancy is always appropriate and can hold and mediate any and all fears and strains in the school situation. The next case balances this optimistic outlook and suggests that there are times when consultancy cannot be adequate to the particular distress in a school situation.

RYESDON C OF E PRIMARY SCHOOL

Conflict over differences of personal commitment

This small voluntary aided school serves the population of two large villages, about five miles from a large town. The school specified no religious requirements for admission and from its inception had served all the people of the locality. The buildings were erected late in the last century. Though it had been upgraded, with the addition of an entrance hall and indoor plumbing, there was a severe shortage of space for the 126 pupils. A class was permanently based in the school hall, which was also the dining room, and the tiny staffroom was required to do double duty as an office. The church next door was in the process of redesigning its interior so that the premises could be of more use to the school. There were 126 pupils and six staff. The staff had been together for a long time, the most recent member arriving twelve years before.

CREATE was invited to help the staff develop its RE in relation to a set of diocesan guidelines which the Head had helped to develop. After the work had been organized, the Head announced that he was moving on to another position. It was evident that project work was a going-away gift to encourage developments in the school, which he had been unable to make during his tenure.

The task specified – working with diocesan RE guidelines – looked safe enough in principle. However, the central question of the guidelines – Who am I? Where am I going? What ought I to do? – were institutional dynamite. They surfaced contentious issues in relation to the future of the Church of England, the identity and purpose of the church school, and educational priorities in the light of the emergent national curriculum. The county had a high proportion of church schools (50 per cent), and as one teacher remarked:

> 'If a teacher moves into this area, they know to dust off their confirmation certificate if they want a job. Being a teacher and being a church member almost goes together in this part of the world.'
>
> *(Fieldnote)*

Staff members all expressed adherence to the Church of England but they framed their beliefs and expressed their spirituality very differently, reflecting the broad nature of that church.

> 'I attended a Catholic convent school as a child and that made a big impression on me and the way I see religion and the Church of England.'
>
> *(Fieldnote)*

> 'I am an evangelical and I worry about "smells and bells". My faith centres on the Bible. Biblical studies was my special subject in college and I think that should be at the centre of RE here.'
>
> *(Fieldnote)*

Church allegiance was not an employment convenience here, but a matter of deep individual conviction. The word 'individual' is used here quite deliberately, because the staff saw anything to do with religion as belonging to the realm of the personal and the private. They found it difficult to make headway with RE work because of a reluctance to talk about personal commitments in a professional context.

Their Flight from the challenges of RE development was a response to the fear that talk of religion would start a row which would irreparably damage working relations. The Flight pattern was reinforced by individual staff skirmishes with the consultant which purported to be about religion. The group were reminding themselves that religion was dragon-occupied territory. But from time to time there was reference to their insecurities.

> 'We know we are a church school and say that is what has held us together for all these years. We can't dig up the ground we're standing on to examine the foundations while we rely on them to hold us up. There may be nothing there, then what do we do?'
>
> *(Fieldnote)*

At one stage, this group developed a pattern of smoothing over disagreements which threatened to surface by making humorous connections to events and discussions at the Church of England Synod, taking place at the time. So a female teacher's criticism of a male colleague's teaching aims was met with the comment,

> 'The next thing you know, she'll be wanting ordination.'
>
> *(Fieldnote)*

Another teacher's affection for 'high Church' liturgical practices drew the remark,

'I don't know what the happy clappies down at Church House would make of that.'

(Fieldnote)

All of the jokes turned on the same two-edged device, that whatever was said was potentially offensive to an individual in the school and a faction on the national church scene. Whatever was said was divisive. Staff appeared unsure of having shared religious positions. Television interviews with bishops each night of the Synod concentrated on identifying the factors which would maintain or destroy Church unity.

If the staff resisted examination of RE principles in an effort to preserve their unity, they could not repress irritating questions about the relevance and the role of the church school.

'It's sometimes difficult to know what the Church school is about when only five of the pupils are at church on a Sunday.'

(Fieldnote)

When these doubts surfaced a specific anxiety, a Flight leader could always be found who would forestall rational work on it.

'It's a waste of time to be spending so much time on RE when it's clear from GERBIL that it's Science and Maths we should be concentrating on. They really matter to parents and inspectors.'

(Fieldnote)

The consultant had not responded to pressure to become a trainer who imported novel RE teaching approaches and resources into the class-room.

'Never mind about what we think and believe, just give me something that I can do with my class tomorrow. That would be a good use of time. It's not up to us to solve the problems of the Church and education.'

(Fieldnote)

It's one thing to rule problems out of bounds. It does not erase them from consciousness.

The RE development meetings continued after the departure of the initiating headteacher. With the arrival of the next Head, a term later, it was time to take stock of events. The project had revealed the fragility of the staff and their reluctance to create roles in relation to RE development. The incoming Head needed a period of hassle-free time to establish himself in the job. So it was decided to end the exercise. In retrospect it is clear that all the circumstances in this case made it an inauspicious time to raise RE issues.

Who am I? Where am I going? What ought I to do? These questions appeared at first glance tailor-made to reinforce the individualistic approach to religion and Religious Education that the staff employed. However, the responses to the questions offered by the diocesan guidelines were based on the shared identity of an established faith tradition. The chosen focus for work brought the staff face to face with their own inability to say 'we'.

Though significant issues were flagged:

1.   fears about variety within a shared religious identity;
2.   the relation between personal faith and RE;
3.   the role of the church school in a secular context;

they could not be taken up by the staff. The school may have been better served by beginning collegial development work with a curriculum area that would not have harnessed so much insecurity. Perhaps these larger issues can be looked at again when the staff have a clear experience of themselves as a united team, able to make, share and implement common policy.

Our own words and images can come back to haunt us in unexpected ways. After all the angst and talk about the danger and folly of investigating 'the nature of the school's foundation', 'the foundations of faith', and the 'fundamental principles of RE', the floors of two of the school's four class-rooms fell in.

FEAR OF FRACTION

The Ryesdon C of E case study shows the way in which people defend personal commitments against the modification of others. This makes it difficult to do fruitful development work in the professional setting. Professional development presents adults with personal challenges and can encourage people to establish new connections in their private interpretive frameworks. This can require changes in formative beliefs and values which are sustained by considerable emotional investment. If the price of professional learning is destruction of a personal world-view, then the danger of collegial curriculum work is evident.

Staff in this school wanted to behave as if there were no differences between their personal and professional lives as far as religion was concerned. They could not make and take the role of RE teacher because they were afraid that it was not possible to fill that role with shared meanings and actions. But they could not ignore questions of religious identity because external pressures from diocese and synod stimulated the need for a corporate expression of the school's religious foundation. The demands were experienced as threatening to tear the school apart. The anxieties raised inside this 'Head-less' group of four could not be addressed. Like rabbits caught in headlights they were paralysed.

The art of RE curriculum development lies in tapping into the values and commitments of participants to energize work in the service of pupils. It is only the memories, enthusiasms, stories and beliefs of the people who take up the teacher role that can serve to expand or critique role behaviour and activities. Strong feelings and passionately held personal beliefs cannot be kept off the overt agenda of professional renewal.

In this case the staff generated persecutory attitudes amongst themselves. In other situations teachers can collude in projecting these onto external agents, powerfully able to influence their future.

ST BENEDICT'S RC PRIMARY SCHOOL

Responding to differences in the local context

St Benedict's is a town-centre school staffed by eight teachers serving 157 pupils. It is next to the parish church which shares its name. One of the priests of the parish, an Irishman and former contemplative monk, is the chairman of governors.

The school is a welcoming place and the staff enjoy good relationships among themselves, organizing social events to mark occasions like birthdays and holidays. The building is old add lacks facilities. The camaraderie and co-operation of the staff is described by them as an aspect of the Dunkirk spirit, necessary to make the poor conditions bearable. The headteacher is proud of the pleasant, caring atmosphere which makes for happy staff and pupils. On prominent display in the staffroom is a clock given as a present by two students who had done a teaching practice in the school. The figures on the dial are written one-ish, two-ish, etc. It is regarded as honouring the human face and pace of a school which is suspicious of rigidity and tight boundaries.

The religious profile of St Benedict's shows there to be 10 per cent practising Catholics out of the 30 per cent who held RC baptismal certificates. Of the remaining 70 per cent of pupils, 63 per cent were Muslims who attend mosque school with the remainder being Hindu. English is a second language for many of the school pupils and language support is provided through the LEA Multi-ethnic Group Support (MEGS) service. Many of the school pupils are the first members of their family to be born in Britain. This echoed an element present at the foundation of the school, which had been set up to provide education for the children of Irish Catholic immigrants in the late 1800s.

The school served the children of families called Brady, O'Neill, Nolan and Kelly up to the mid-1970s. Then a movement of Catholic families to the suburbs of the town led to Asian families occupying the older terraced housing in the St Benedict's catchment area. The school kept up its pupil numbers by admitting pupils from the locality, irrespective of their faith adherence. The religious profile of the school developed as a consequence of this unexamined policy. In 1987 some school governors saw this situation as anomalous and argued that the school be closed on the grounds that it was no longer a Catholic school.

The Head and staff agreed to pursue RE development work, with consultant support, designed to find out more about Islam and introduce a multifaith element into the course offerings. But the real issue processed in the project was the survival of the school, given the demographic changes and questions about what makes a Catholic school Catholic. The staff presented themselves as under seige from external, traditional forces set on Catholic schools for Catholic pupils. A neighbouring diocese had stated such a policy and current publications from the Bishops' Educational Commission suggested that it was difficult to maintain a Catholic ethos in a school which had over 20 per cent non-Catholic pupils.

> 'We feel so isolated. No one from outside is giving us any help. People going to and from the church next door deliberately raise their voices so that we can hear the racist remarks that they make. The children hear them too.'
>
> *(Fieldnote)*

The behaviour of the chairman of governors, who was also the school chaplain, was seen as counter-productive.

> 'Fr Michael never touches them [the Asian pupils] or talks to them when he comes in. It's like they don't exist. If he had his way I suspect that none of us, Catholic or Asian, pupil or teacher, would be here.'
>
> *(Fieldnote)*

Church custom in education at home and abroad was compared.

'I sent my money off to the nuns in mission countries when I was at school. Now I realize that they were not running Catholic schools for Catholic pupils. They were teaching Maths to Muslims. So now I ask why what they do in Pakistan is such a worthy activity when it's so suspect if we do the equivalent in Britain.'

(Fieldnote)

As the staff began to catalogue those they now caricatured as potential enemies – governors, clergy and co-religionists – they had to confront the strategies they had used to keep their critics at bay. This included maintaining a curriculum which had Mass attendance as a compulsory component and an assembly programme which used exclusively Christian forms of worship, addressing God in trinitarian terms. The talk about caring for the traditions and values of non-Catholic pupils masked a real expectation that they could happily inhabit the practices of their Roman Catholic peers. Asian failure to fulfil these expectations was interpreted as a discipline problem.

'The older boys are very badly behaved in assembly. They won't pray. And I thought their religion was supposed to have great respect for prayer.'

(Fieldnote)

The attitudes staff criticized in governors, clergy, and church educational directives were apparent in their own policies. They were the ones who obliged Muslims to go to Mass and required them to address God as Father, Son and Holy Spirit, a blasphemy against the unity of God in the teachings of Islam.

During the consultancy there was a painful and gradual withdrawal of negative projections from outside agencies so that staff could confront their own ambivalence about the religious convictions of the pupil population. This achieved strong focus in one teacher's tearful outburst.

'So now I've learned something new. Mass is bad for some people and I should stop thinking it's good, or at least will do them no harm. What's out there is in me too. Don't get me wrong. I love the kids, but I sometimes do a double-take and wonder if this is a Catholic school. I'm not sure it is anymore.'

(Fieldnote)

Other staff members could see in this heartfelt expression the source of their own ambiguous feelings when faced with the task of bringing together school tradition and the religious educational needs of all their pupils.

> The truth we sought elsewhere is in ourselves,
> Yet not there either, for we know by halves
> Even our own wishes. How can we know
> Others', and still less others who, like us,
> Are blind and hopeful, and impervious
> To all words not their own, and find us so?

C. H. Sisson, 'Sonnet'[6]

Caught in the middle of confusion, mixed motives and false perceptions, people worried that changes in practice would not be understandable, acceptable or even explicable to outsiders.

Talk of 'them' and 'us' moderated, but the Dependent attitudes which had led the staff to apply an inappropriate and punishing liturgical regime proved more resistant to recognition.

'A lot of us have swallowed a lot of old catechism answers. "Outside the church there is no salvation" and all that. There is a lot of pre-Vatican I stuff in us, though we would like to think of ourselves as Vatican II types.'

(Fieldnote)

They represented themselves as children fed indigestible dinners, fastened into old-fashioned garments to restrict their movements. The consultant suggested that the group had internalized a punitive image of Mother Church. Some agreed that this may have accounted for their inability to act like competent educational professionals. One teacher described the paralysis in terms of her adolescent children.

'We are caught in the pinch between a secure past and an uncertain future, and we are being thoroughly adolescent about it. We don't know what to do for the best so we don't do anything and wait for somebody else to sort it out. But that may sort us out of a job. Deciding not to decide is a decision. And besides all this, the Asian pupils are badly served despite all our big words about tolerance and caring.'

(Fieldnote)

They had acknowledged and taken responsibility for the negative feelings about teaching in a multifaith situation that they had foisted onto others. Now they had to recover a good, 'nurturing' mother element in Church and educational tradition so that fears and resentments about a possible school closure could be tackled.

The work in this school was kept on the boil by a group of four staff, who saw value and integrity in the consultancy process.

'What is so good about this is that we get some time and space to do all this talking and listening so that we can discover what's really bugging us. If we are brave enough we can come up with some useful activity for a positive future.'

(Fieldnote)

The project became nicknamed 'Time and Space' as staff realized its utility as a structure for serious work on their situation, which freed day-to-day life from an all-pervading pall of worry.

Recovering strands in the tradition of 'Mother' Church, which valued religious liberty, education as a human good and justice for all, they were able to begin discussions with diocesan agencies about the future. This used the energies of the Dependency Assumption towards activity in the real world, and handled the survival issues through mature work and building an alliance with the diocesan RE adviser.

They were reassured that no pre-emptive action for closure would be taken by the governors and were encouraged to develop RE approaches more appropriate to the experience of the pupils. Staff produced a new RE policy document and class-room work began to turn the principles into programmes of study. This received encouragement when the LEA film unit videoed an RE class to demonstrate good practice in multi-ethnic educational settings. With this positive endorsement from an external agency, the wheel appeared to have turned full circle.

At the beginning of the next academic year the consultant visited the school. There had been an influx of Catholic pupils across the whole age range as the result of the reactivation and refurbishment of some high-rise housing near the school. The families, relocated to this accommodation from all parts of the county, had a history of social deprivation. The school had to respond to new relational and behavioural difficulties.

A significant number of ethnic minority pupils transferred to other schools. One teacher remarked:

'Well, last year we were all hot and bothered about religion and education. Now I'm getting myself resigned to being a social worker. I have to feed some in my class before I can teach them.'

(Fieldnote)

Another pointed out that

'All that work we did with you doesn't seem very relevant to the new intake. But at least we now have a way of working together to identify the real needs of pupils. We got it right last year, I suppose we can do it again.'

(Fieldnote)

THE RENEWAL PROCESS

The St Benedict's story raises some significant dynamics in the renewal process. The stimulus for development can often be perceived as an agonizing invasion of the alien.

> . . . pain like an assault,
> The old pain again
> When the world thrusts itself inside,
> When we have to take in the outside,
> When we have to decide
> To be crazy-human with hope
> Or just plain crazy
> With fear.
>
> *May Sarton, 'Night Watch'*[7]

The decision for hope or fear is not made once only. The group remains in a continual state of emotional flux. It is an indicator of the condition of the group.

> We tend to constantly go back and forwards between states of mind where we feel primarily frightened, persecuted, aggrieved, complaining and bearing a grudge against those who do not provide for us in the way we would wish – or primarily caring, appreciative of others and taking responsibility for our contribution to the difficult situations in which we find ourselves.[8]

This oscillation shows that belief in linear development is a lie. The adage that 'every day in every way things are getting better and better' is testimony to the triumph of optimism over experience. Some of the literature on change written in the 1980s argued that making change was merely a problem of the efficient administration of a structured programme. Such a rational and logical approach fails to attend to the passions and values which surface in moments of institutional destabilization. These can be valuable, revealing alternative ways to think about a situation. Would St Benedict's Asian pupils have been really helped if their RE curriculum had a multifaith dimension while they were still required to attend Mass and make the sign of the cross? Simplicity and rigidity in the structure of development exercises can be counter-productive. Wendell Berry comments on structures, saying:

. . . form serves us best when it works as an obstruction to baffle us and deflect our intended course. It may be that when we no longer know what to do, we have come to our real work and that when we no longer know which way to go we have begun our real journey. The mind that is not baffled is not employed. The impeded stream is the one that sings.[9]

The notion of impediments, limits and barriers to free actions was a salient feature of work in this school. It illustrates the powerful effect which the aims and interests of other people such as churches, LEAs and housing departments can exert upon school life. They exist beyond the boundaries of the school but are also resident in the minds of staff in idealized, introjected or projected forms.

The next chapter pays special attention to boundary management in the presentation of schools involved in more complex 'political' interactions with partners in the educational enterprise.

NOTES AND REFERENCES

1. In *The Bloodaxe Book of Contemporary Women Poets* (1985), ed. J. Couzyn (Newcastle upon Tyne: Bloodaxe Books), p. 135.
2. *Poems 1913–1956*, edited by J. Willet and R. Maheim (1987) (London: Methuen), pp. 378–9.
3. A. K. Rice (1965) 'Learning for leadership', in A. D. Colman and W. H. Bexton (eds), *Group Relations Reader* (Washington, DC: A. J. Rice Institute).
4. R. J. Alexander (1984) *Primary Teaching* (London: Cassell), p. 188.
5. Atwood, M. (1984) 'The Sin Eater', in *Dancing Girls and Other Stories* (London: Virago), p. 213.
6. *First and Always*, edited by L. Snail (1988) (London: Faber & Faber), p. 62.
7. *A Grain of Mustard Seed – New Poems* (1971) (New York: W. W. Norton), p. 29.
8. I. Salzeberger-Wittenberg (1983) 'The Emotional Aspects of Learning' in I. Salzberger-Wittenberg, G. Henry and E. Osborne *The Emotional Experience of Learning and Teaching* (London: Routledge & Kegan Paul), p. 68.
9. W. Berry (1983) *Standing by Words* (San Francisco: Northpoint Press), p. 205.

Chapter 8

Politics and Pluralism

> From time to time in human affairs
> Facts give way to fiction
> To do one thing we believe many things
> And if for a time we believe fictions
> The fact that we are humans
> Gives way to the fiction that we are monsters
> And when we live in fiction we pay in fact
> Later when we look at the stones and broken bones
> We wonder how we ever believed such lies!
> We are not evil
> But because we desire others to be happy
> We are cruel
> If we believe fictions we sink in corruption
> And the corruption of the living
> Is worse than the corruption of the dead
> Who only breathe into our nostrils
> But cannot act
>
> *Edward Bond, 'Sonnet 10'*[1]

One of the most difficult boundaries to recognize is the fine line between truth and lies. Standard rhetoric attributes mendacity to others who 'bend the truth', 'don't tell the full story' and 'juggle the figures'. Brute lies are always attributed to others. Our own experience shows how easily issues become blurred, so that in soft focus fact fades imperceptibly into more convenient fiction. Short-sightedness is humankind's available protection against too much perception. This strategy of denial uses degrees of blindness as a tactic in the battle against disturbing reality.

Bond's poem draws attention to the consequences of the immature desire to keep everybody happy and secure. It points up the sterility of a future inspired by the stale breath of the past. New actions depend upon seeing things differently. Blinkered people collude in the lie that old behaviour remains useful in changed circumstances. Unable to think second thoughts, they reject current insights and organize the future as if they possessed all the resources to save the day. Strategies for salvation are enacted with a backward and reverent glance to solutions to past problems. People are ready to be seduced into accepting that the formulae which met historical needs remain relevant to present difficulties. The following case studies illustrate the dangers of this comfortable assumption.

RICHMOND ROAD COUNTY PRIMARY

Undermining differences by the provision of an imposed programme

Richmond Road is a large school, half a mile from the bright lights of the promenade attractions of a major seaside resort. Many of the pupils' families are involved in the tourism business, some as hoteliers and restaurateurs, others as service staff. Some families only stay for a season, housed in bed and breakfast accommodation, hopeful of finding work. This gives the school a large transient population. Though the school had 790 pupils on roll at any given time, 512 pupils left the school in 1987.

The school is accommodated in a three-storey building typical of turn-of-the-century school architecture, and has small playgrounds surrounded by high iron railings. Though there is a lot of exposed concrete and red brick, the stairwell and corridors are brightly decorated with childrens' work. This school is one of the largest in the area and there are 28 staff.

The initial staff meeting attended by 22 staff, surfaced clear indications of the plurality of thought and practice present in the school.

> 'If I'm honest, I do RE in the most general way, as a dimension of topic work. I don't know much about religion myself. It seems to cause a lot of trouble in the world and in school.'
>
> *(Fieldnote)*

> 'It's very important that children have a firm moral base. That's where RE comes in. RE is for the Ten Commandments, not the Koran brigade.'
>
> *(Fieldnote)*

> 'The real test of RE in a school is, do you see the pupils pleasanter and better behaved for it?'
>
> *(Fieldnote)*

> 'It's important that children have knowledge about the religions of other people, if they are going to understand them and get on with them.'
>
> *(Fieldnote)*

The teachers were pleased to get all of this 'off their chests'. They had a desire for a more coherent school-wide RE practice, but saw the size of the group as impractical for achieving that aim. There was swift and general agreement that it was better undertaken by a working party of self-selected volunteers, in cooperation with the RE curriculum co-ordinator and a Deputy Head. The meeting concluded optimistically with participants congratulating themselves on the streamlined administrative approach adopted to launch the venture.

This confidence was somewhat at odds with the experience of the first working party meeting. There was a general fog about the purpose and authority of the group. Some people were there as representatives of the factions which had spoken at the meeting. Others were there for professional development with an outside trainer. Some thought they had been mandated to work on a practical programme on 'friendship' which would improve playground discipline. There was a suggestion that they were to think through RE policy on behalf of the others, however people were dubious about doing other people's thinking for them.

The group was in the position of the rider in the fable, who attempted to ride a horse which had not been properly broken in. As soon as the horse felt the weight in the saddle he bucked and bolted, careering headlong down the road. When a friend of the hapless jockey called after him, 'Where are you off to?', pointing to the horse he replied, 'Don't ask me, ask the bloody horse.'

The working party couldn't get a grip on the problem because it had neither a clear aim nor real authority to act. They had been sent off with the impossible task of creating harmony between people uninvolved in the reconciling process. The hastily convened group was less about work than maintaining a social defence against the anxiety of staff disagreement. As long as the RE group were meeting and talking, the staff as a whole could enjoy an illusory confidence that harmony was just round the corner. Carrying the burden of these expectations put the working party into considerable panic as they attempted to turn the fantasies of their peers into solid proposals for activity. They expressed frustration at their own inability to identify pupil learning needs and develop a programme to meet them. Whatever was nominated for attention was quickly abandoned as appearing to represent only one element of the staff. If it would please multifaithers, how would the 'moralists' or 'the Christians' view it? If the 'citizenship lobby' were impressed would the 'traditionalists' recognize it as RE?

In choosing to pursue 'mission impossible' – to come up with something that would keep everybody happy, totally renewing the situation without changing anything – the group had set itself up for disappointment. The consultant invited the group to consider how the whole staff were using the working party to handle RE discomfort. But this was rejected as irrelevant. The real need was to show that the working party was a 'good group' by producing something for others to use.

Christmas provided a short-term and safe focus for activity. Only Scrooge and process consultants could be against Christmas! The group worked to produce an approach to Christmas across the 4–11 age range, offering a four-week scheme of work to each staff member. This was presented to colleagues one afternoon after school with an exhibition of books and resources appropriate to the programme. Half of the staff turned up to discuss the work over a glass of wine and the event left the working group feeling very good.

> 'It's good that so many turned up to see the stuff. They seem pleased to have a practical activity for the classroom.'

> *(Fieldnote)*

January brought great changes. The RE curriculum co-ordinator had left the school for another post and another teacher was temporarily filling the post. Teachers, after school commitments, sports fixtures, medical appointments, family crises, wedding arrangements, and other staff meetings, cut attendance at the monthly meeting. No one person was present at all of the last eight sessions, one was present at six, another at five. Sometimes people sent substitutes who were unfamiliar with events and irritated founder members by talking in terms of the aim of the exercise as they variously remembered it from the previous summer. The group was haemorrhaging personnel and enthusiasm and had lost all boundaries of time, membership and task.

It was as if the Christmas material had justified the group's existence and the membership decided to quit while they were ahead. There was also a recognition, born out of the presence of the newcomers, that the group had lost touch with the expectations of the staff. To remedy this a questionnaire was circulated to colleagues asking them to specify both their understanding of RE and the aims of the development exercise. Only seven forms were returned, indicating that not even those on the working party had completed this task. The RE co-ordinator and the Deputy Head found themselves fronting an enterprise which had lost support. There was talk of a loss of direction and black humour about the RE group as curriculum martyrs thrown into the staff meeting arena.

> 'It seems that we were set up to fail. While we've been working, the rest of the staff have had totally unrealistic ideas about our achievement. Being in this group, I feel I've drawn the short straw.'
>
> *(Fieldnote)*

In an effort to avoid being mauled by their peers because of inactivity or perceived professional incompetence, the co-ordinator and Deputy set a new task of RE syllabus production. Though they had not been delegated to do this, it was thought that the staff would be grateful and suitably impressed.

Syllabus design usually follows from an agreed statement of curriculum policy. Efforts to develop shared policy in the working group was seen as time-consuming and frustrating.

> 'I'm not sure that any of this is useful to people outside this group. We might learn from it here, but when it gets into a policy document it's just more new stuff to misunderstand and misapply. If people have not been present during its development, they'll not take ownership of it. But if we give them clear guidelines on the way syllabus content ties in with existing topic work that will be an immediately useful framework for their thinking.'
>
> *(Fieldnote)*

The group encouraged Pairing between the Deputy and acting RE co-ordinator, who ran about convening mini meetings which planned RE around existing curriculum offerings. There was an atmosphere of accomplishment.

> 'You see what we can achieve when we really get going.'
>
> *(Fieldnote)*

But there was a distinctly empty feel to some of the chat. One comment, described as jaundiced by other members, proved startlingly prophetic.

> 'Of course they [the rest of the staff] are too polite to rubbish our efforts. They'll tell us we've done well and quietly not use the material. Let's face it, RE is a low priority because it's not in the core curriculum. And I'm not sure what we've produced will meet the expectations of the rest.'
>
> *(Fieldnote)*

The syllabus notes never made it into a final typed draft for the school curriculum file and no further work was done.

REPRESENTATION AND OWNERSHIP

The delegation of small working groups to address an issue on behalf of a larger group is regarded as an efficient way of expediting results. But as the Richmond Road experience demonstrates, the representation of others is fraught with questions about the status and power of the few invited to make proposals on the future activity of the many.

If the working party is made up of delegates who are to represent the conflicting interests within the larger staff, it is unlikely that progress will be made. However, it may not be clear that the whole staff have given members of the working group authority to use their full discretion and independent judgement in pursuing their endeavours. The larger group can feel betrayed by a group which has developed new internal loyalties, beyond the remit apparent at its inception. The politics of representation bedevil any curriculum development exercises structured around working parties.

> An academy, like a business firm or government agency, is a political system of partly conflicting interests in which decisions are made through bargaining power and coalition formation. In general there appears to be a few elementary rules of operating in a political system. Power comes from a favourable position for trading favours. Thus it comes from the possession of resources and the idiosyncrasy of preferences, from valuing things that others do not and having things that others value. If you do not have them, get them – even if you don't value them yourself.[2]

The Richmond Road working group tried to offer valued resources. But when the small group came to question the validity of doing other people's lesson planning and identified the need for a comprehensive RE policy-making role, they lost one constituency and failed to find a new one. It was a case of one group's learning outstripping the pace of another's development. With no adequate communication structure to keep working party and staff group in touch with each other, the marginalization of the working group was inevitable.

Unable to understand the work that had been done and why it took the form it did, the staff could not appropriate it. The small group was seen to have exceeded its authority, laboured and brought forth a gnat. Had they resisted the flight into activity and put more thought into the aim, role and authority of the working group and its relationship to the staff as a whole, the teachers would have been able to work with greater freedom.

The issue of authority and freedom to work is manifest in the strained external relations of the next school.

ST PETER'S RC PRIMARY SCHOOL

Suppression of differences about educational and eccelesial tradition

St Peter's RC is a small, light and well-designed school, two miles from town C which has a large ethnic minority population. The school was built to serve the Catholic children of the neighbouring middle-class villages, though it attracts a few pupils from town-centre parishes whose schools admit Asian pupils. There are 185 pupils and eight staff.

The school is part of a Catholic diocese which had a policy of Catholic schools for Catholic pupils. The diocese steers a separate course from the majority of others in the country in regard to sacramental and educational policy.

The present school staff has been in post together for the last twelve years and wanted something new to happen. The Head also wanted a 'breath of fresh air' into the school. Familiarity had made things a little stale and he was keen to explore possibilities for achieving staff development through curriculum development. Since he described RE as the *raison d'être* of the school, the linchpin of curriculum, school ethos and culture, it appeared a natural place to begin any development work. The progress of the consultancy was to reveal the extent to which the lifestyles of staff and relations with the diocese made RE in the school difficult to deal with.

From the outset, it proved difficult to arrange meeting times with the teachers as two of the three women on the staff had young children and needed to leave at 4.15 to pick them up from babysitters. Since 90-minute sessions after school were impossible, the meetings were rescheduled into 60-minute slots, many of which took place over lunch breaks. Two longer sessions took place on appointed INSET days.

One such meeting appeared to get the work off to a reflective and positive start with the teachers building a collective picture of the school and the contextual factors influencing its Religious Education policies. The staff saw themselves confronting a tide of greed and commercialism which was eroding the spiritual values that the school represented.

> 'I suppose it's the 1980s ethos: have, get, spend, possess, own is the game. And if you can't afford to play, you're a failure. You can see that competitive attitude in some of the children here.'
>
> *(Fieldnote)*

Though the teachers were disturbed by this attitude, they were not sure that they were effective in changing it.

> 'The children say all the right things about caring and sharing and loving and helping. It's sad that they can't put it into practice with one another.'
>
> *(Fieldnote)*

The pastoral and educational plans of the diocese had significantly affected RE in the school. The policy of building up co-operation between home and school and parish raised ambivalent feelings in the staff. As parents, they recognized and supported the logic of collaboration, but as teachers they experienced the changes as a loss of authority. Switching sacramental preparation for First Communion from school to parish had left staff unclear as to their role in the faith development of pupils.

> 'It was sad to see it [sacramental preparation] go. It was considered an honour to teach the First Communion class. And it was always called that, not top infants. I thought that it brought school and parish together. Now preparation takes place in the parish with catechists and we don't know much about it.'
>
> *(Fieldnote)*

> 'It's a bit of a cheek to ask the Head to train volunteer catechists in how to deal with young children. When you've got a staffroom full of dogs it doesn't make much sense to teach the rest of the menagerie to bark badly.'
>
> *(Fieldnote)*

Uncertainty about their role in pupils' religious formation meant that the RE pro-gramme was a hotchpotch of ideas and enthusiasms.

'We don't really have a set RE syllabus. It has grown out of a lot of experiment with English, Irish and American catechetical material, blended together to suit our needs.'

(Fieldnote)

But the Head was clear that they were concerned with religious nurture, education for confessional commitment rather than wide-ranging knowledge.

'As a Catholic school we exist to develop the faith of pupils, and RE here focuses on the gospel stories and the doctrines of the Church.'

(Fieldnote)

This concentration on the ecclesial community meant that other faith traditions were not given curricular space.

'We could just as well be in the middle of Suffolk as in C. We don't touch other religions. It's a bit odd really, because a lot of these children will go to secondary school at St Augustine's, in the centre of town, which takes Asians. We seem to be saying that other races and faiths are irrelevant, but next autumn these children will be sitting next to Mumtaz and Prakesh in school.'

(Fieldnote)

During this opening session the Head was often absent, 'attending to other business'. He explained his sudden departures as giving the staff more freedom to talk, though he appeared to disagree with and disapprove of a lot of what they said in front of him. He had worries, which he did not share with the staff, about the difficulty of demonstrat-ing traditional, Catholic family values when half of the staff were divorced. The women talked openly about this in an exploration of the changing middle-class experience of Catholicism.

'Some of the children here are living in second families and our falling rolls are the direct consequence of the use of birth control. Two of us here are divorced. So it's not like it used to be. There are good aspects to that, but it's also confusing when you are trying to set your Catholic stall out.'

(Fieldnote)

The staff were in a situation of cultural and ethical confusion similar to that described by Matthew Arnold. For them there was

> neither joy, nor love, nor light,
> Nor certitude, nor peace, nor help for pain;
> And we are here as on a darkling plain
> Swept with confused alarms of struggle and flight,
> Where ignorant armies clash by night.
>
> *Matthew Arnold, 'Dover Beach'*[3]

Despite the Head's worries and the women's confusion, the staff avoided any embarrass-ing examination of the ambiguities of Catholic living.

Each of us needs to establish some sense of identity and unity in order to give coherence to the multifariousness of our history as uniquely ours and as constitutive of the self. Self-deception can accompany this need for unity, as we systematically delude ourselves in order to maintain the story that has hitherto assured our identity. We hesitate to spell out certain engagements when spelling them out would jeopardize the set of avowals we have made about ourselves.[4]

They saw their options restricted by a diocese committed to a conservative vision. This definitely ruled out work on religious pluralism and the RE needs of the pupils.

'Children need to have a strong religious identity before they are encouraged to ask questions or look at the faith of others. That's for the secondary school.'

(Fieldnote)

The fear of Church disapproval was clear when a diocesan adviser attended a meeting at the school. At the best of times the staff found it difficult to work. On this occasion, terrified of saying the wrong thing in front of a putative ally whom they experienced as the enemy, the staff clammed up. Their behaviour had all the timidity of Eliot's women of Canterbury, who succeeded in living quietly without attracting attention. They lacked confidence in their diocesan masters but had no wish to incur their imagined wrath. They had to make a decision about handling the development exercise that would safely preserve the status quo.

> Difficult to decide? To know what you want?
> How can the puppet tell what the master's hands will do next?
> Some decisions are considered painstakingly – then you do what's best
> The others? Do it! – Then you learn who you are
> These are the decisions by which you live

Edward Bond, 'Deciding'[5]

It was as if they could not withdraw from the consultancy without revealing their curriculum cowardice, so they decided to run the initiative up a blind alley. The Flight from RE development work was hidden by a decision to use the exercise to improve the Friday afternoon assemblies, attended by all pupils and some parents. These events were described by the Head as crucial to home-school communication. This was hard to believe given the unavailability of the majority of parents at 3 p.m. In restricting the consultancy focus to the last event of the school week, after the formal end of classes, the staff were hinting at their desire for its banishment.

Ironically, concentration on this public boundary, which celebrated school identity, illuminated the role of religion at St Peter's. The Head insisted that the assemblies follow the Sunday readings in the lectionary. This dependency on a liturgical manual controlled the way biblical material was used, restricting connections between the Gospel and experience.

'The Church's readings give us everything we need and the stories have a fixed meaning. You can't just let children or anyone else make what they want out of the Bible. The Church has fixed the meanings of these stories. We've got to teach these meanings.'

(Fieldnote)

The unstated rules governing these events were clearly understood by everyone. These para-liturgical celebrations were not about discomforting Gospel challenges or questions about ways of being in the world. When the Feast of Christ the King was celebrated, it was considered fine to depict Christ surrounded by people of all races and colours. However, a poster showing the cross in company with the symbols of other faiths was taken down because it was 'giving credibility to paganism'.

The assemblies were to hand on inherited understandings to a new generation and served to reassure parents present that the religious ethos of the school was about repetition and maintenance of the old ways. The INSET work which won approval were suggestions for show business razzamatazz to pep up the usual assembly formula. The school chaplain had had a theatrical career before ordination and supported this 'let's do the show right here' approach. Creative energies were expended on the style rather than the purpose or pedagogy of these assemblies.

Even though the staff knew that their presentation of ecclesial identity was anachronistic, they organized their assemblies as if there were no questions about inherited patterns of behaviour. This disengagement from present experience and rational thought ensured that the Friday celebrations remained the twilight zone of the week. This was an excellent defence against their worries about clerical criticisms. No one was likely to take them to task for giving traditional irrelevance a face-lift.

TASK, FREEDOM AND AUTHORITY

Central to the teacher's role is the freedom and authority to undertake responsible professional activity to help pupils make sense of the world. The staff at St Peter's readily accepted that their self-limitations and inability to act came from diocesan and clerical pressures. Though they were half-ready to admit that their pupils ought to be educated to live and work alongside Asian children, they retreated from the challenge. Curricular contradictions of this sort have been explored by Agyris and Schon.

> When someone is asked how he would behave under certain circumstances, the answer he usually gives is his espoused theory of action for that situation. This is the theory of action to which he gives allegiance and which, upon request, he communicates to others. However the theory that actually governs his actions is his theory-in-use, which may or may not be compatible with his espoused theory; furthermore, the individual may or may not be aware of the incompatibility of the two theories.[6]

The staff group in this school were well aware of the gulf between good intentions and actual practice, explaining their behaviour with cavalier assertions that 'it is more than my job's worth to do otherwise'. This accounted for the undercurrent of antagonism towards the consultant, who was a reflective witness to this failure of nerve. The high value CREATE placed on the testing and transcending of limitations ran counter to the values of compliance embedded in the school culture. In this situation staff considered it prudent to present a familiar pattern of knowledge despite nagging doubts about the threadbare nature of some inherited values.

Lurking behind the image of diocese as Big Brother was a more domestic fear of discovering the value and lifestyle differences of staff members. It was a case of 'We have seen the enemy and he is us'. The group were afraid that the staff's espoused positions may be at variance with official Church teaching. In a Roman Catholic staff group of four, that would be to name the unnameable.

The struggle to say what can't be said because it reflects badly on the self was a feature of work in another voluntary aided school. In that situation, however, staff found courage to frame their concerns and undertake new action.

ST MARK'S C OF E PRIMARY SCHOOL

Coping with difference over curriculum content

People in town C describe its outlying areas as the White Highlands. St Mark's suburban location, with its mixture of council housing terraces and modern semis, qualifies for this appellation. The school of 185 pupils and eight staff draws its exclusively white intake from the immediate area.

The headteacher is an ordained clergyman who has a special interest in RE, having just completed a Master's degree in the subject. The reluctance of other Church of England schools to take part in the CREATE project prompted him to offer St Mark's participation, though he thought that a school with an ethnically mixed pupil population would have been more representative of the town's Church of England schools.

Since diocesan RE guidelines had been published recently it was natural for the staff to use them as a framework for a review of their own practice. It appeared a safe enough undertaking in a town whose educational community were stressed by issues of race and religion. The illusion of safety vanished during the first exercise, based on the guideline question 'Who am I?' When this was posed to the school in its context, the political and ethical challenges of life in a multicultural community became evident. The session was very lively and the staff were energized by knitting together the factors in town and nation which affected the school, its teachers and pupils.

> 'There's the current educational reforms . . . and funding . . . pupil recruitment – the birth rate . . . the diocesan policies . . . the flat roof . . . our Christian traditions . . . local racism . . . the Asians in town . . . parental expectations . . . good relationships in the school.'
>
> *(Fieldnote)*

The need to educate pupils about the faith and culture of their Asian peers was apparent. A month later the atmosphere had changed.

> 'After you left we started to talk things over and we think we know what's going on. We're getting them [Asians] next year and this religious work is just a way of getting us into it.'
>
> *(Fieldnote)*

The group was caught in a panic about an imagined change in the admissions policy of the school to permit the entry of Asian pupils. This was not the plan but the fantasy highlighted the anxieties of staff, who remained suspicious of the motives of RE development.

The opening exercise had invited them to look beyond the safe environs of the schoolyard and they had taken fright at the variety of pressures upon them in their role of educator. The destabilization in the wider environment reflected changes inside the staff group, which had been together for a number of years. This year retirements, people leaving for promotion, and the hiring of younger staff members meant that relationships, alliances and policies were to be open to revision. The RE work became the focus of staff worries over instability and they expressed resentment at the questions 'Where am I going?' and 'What ought I to do?'

> 'I don't call these guidelines. They are just a load of problems. I expect the diocese to give me answers, not to disturb me with questions when I've got to get on and teach children.'
>
> *(Fieldnote)*

In order to work with the questions in relation to St Mark's situation the staff had to move beyond their Dependency Assumption. May Sarton catches the emotions and behaviour which typify this struggle towards maturity.

> In a state of growth
> We are in pain,
> Violent, hard to live with.
> Our wounds ache.
> We curse rather than bless.

> *May Sarton, 'Night Watch'*[7]

Curses were piled on the diocese, the Head and the consultant before the staff came to appreciate the benefit of working with questions rather than pre-packaged answers. Then they could name the experiences which had fed their anxieties.

'There is a very high incidence of ill health among C of E headteachers in this town who have ethnic minorities in their schools. The staffs are very stressed. I'm not keen on finishing up like that.'

(Fieldnote)

'I've never had any experience of minority pupils, their language and religion and so on. I'm retiring next year and I'm too old for new stuff now.'

(Fieldnote)

'Even if it's just adding some multifaith RE, I don't want to be doing something in a class-room in an experimental way. I want it properly worked through by everyone.'

(Fieldnote)

Resistance now became organized through Flight and mourning for the paradisal days when Christian culture united the whole nation. Any move to sophisticated work threatened to reveal differences over RE, harmful to staff unity. The group were frozen into inactivity by a fear of failure. Whilst this fantasy possessed the staff as an RE development group, co-operative work on the annual pantomime was enthusing the same set of people.

Some Asian pupils from Hill View Primary School had been invited to the show. It was to be the first step in a 'getting to know you' exercise. The pantomime provided the staff group with mixed opportunity for learning. It gave them behavioural evidence of their capacity for flexibility and good-natured co-operation towards a shared task. But accusations about racist remarks made by their pupils to the Hill View children forced them to confront racism in pupils and themselves.

They decided to make racial and religious prejudice an important aspect of the moral and religious teaching offered to children. They were able to draw on the RE expertise of the Head in developing a programme which informed pupils about the faith and values of non-Christian traditions, and focused on issues of equality and justice. The RE working group appeared when the teachers themselves realized they were prepared to face a common challenge.

A work group is born when a number of individuals, bound together by and anxious over the omnipresent image of the dismembered body, manage to overcome this anxiety, to reassure themselves and see and feel themselves as human beings, to feel pleasant, common, positive feelings. These feelings may then give rise to concerted actions and thoughts, enabling them to describe the changes that have overcome them. When they come to feel themselves as 'us'. When a unit superior to each individual, but in which each has a part, comes into being, then the group is born, like a living body. Each person recognises himself as a 'member'. The group that at last functions as such becomes differentiated and organised; the biological metaphor remains all-powerful: it gives itself 'organs' of decision-making, executive functions and control.[8]

THE THRESHOLD OF TRANSFORMATION

This story provides a good example of the discomfort involved in setting aside images that have out-lived their utility. In the case of the St Mark's staff, it was the picture of themselves as an island of white Christian culture under threat, with an accompanying sense of themselves as unable to work together on the challenges of a pluralistic society. It is unlikely that the group would have voluntarily surrendered these understandings which had worked to keep external reality at bay. It took accusations of racism to threaten their idealized, liberal and fair image of themselves and plant an uncomfortable seed of self-suspicion. Events following the pantomime required the renegotiation of their own staff role and the educational mission of the school. In feeling terms this may be experienced as

> The descent
>   made up of despairs
>   and without accomplishment
> realizes a new awakening:
>   which is a reversal
> of despair.

William Carlos Williams, 'The Descent'[9]

Didier Anzieu emphasizes the formative nature of such moments by acknowledging that

the shifting of unconscious images comes about only in crisis situations and through a dramatic process that Hegel tried to conceptualize as aufhaben, i.e. at once to negate, to overcome and to preserve. These preserved images that one has gone beyond, constitute in the end the essential reality of human groups.[10]

This transformation was not a series of individual conversions or changes in attitude. It was the movement of the whole group into new possibilities for thought and action, and relied upon radical collaboration.

> After, when they disentwine
> You from me and yours from mine,
> Neither can be certain who
> Was that I whose mine was you.
> To the act again they go
> More completely not to know.
>
> Theft is theft and raid is raid
> Though reciprocally made.

Robert Graves, 'The Thieves'[11]

This temporary weakening of personal boundaries is a feature of collaborative reconceptualization. Eventually no one can remember who voiced the breakthrough suggestions or who took it up, developed and elaborated it into a practical proposal. But it is always a generative and intimate exchange. In this case, it was based on the teachers' positive experience of working enjoyably together to produce the show. They were building confidently on previous experience, expecting a satisfactory outcome. To borrow a phrase from Bion, they saw the completed and successful event 'casting a shadow before itself'.

In the next chapter this foreshadowing phenomenon reappears, presaging school divisions and breakup as staff struggle with questions of religious and institutional identity.

NOTES AND REFERENCES

1. *Poems 1978–1985* (1987) (London: Methuen), p. 249.
2. J. G. March 'Theories of choice and making decisions', *Social Science and Modern Society* Vol 20, No 1 (1982) (New York: Transaction Inc.), p. 63.
3. *The Poems of Matthew Arnold*, edited by C. B. Tinker and F. H. Lawry (1950) (London: OUP), pp. 210–12.
4. S. Haverwas and D. Burrell (1977) 'Self-deception and autobiography: Reflections on Speer's "Inside the Third Reich"', in *Truthfulness and Tragedy: Further Investigations in Christian Ethics* (Notre Dame, IN: University of Notre Dame Press), p. 87.
5. *Poems 1978–1985* (1987) (London: Methuen), p. 71.
6. C. Agyris and D. Schon (1974) *Theory in Practice* (San Francisco: Jossey-Bass), p. 7.
7. *A Grain of Mustard Seed – New Poems* (1971) (New York: W. W. Norton), p. 29.
8. D. Anzieu (1984) *The Group and the Unconscious* (London: Routledge & Kegan Paul), p. 123.
9. *Penguin Modern Poets 9* (1967) (London: Penguin), p. 117.
10. D. Anzieu, *The Group and the Unconscious*, p. 128.
11. *Collected Poems* (1965) (London: Cassell), p. 156.

Chapter 9

Pattern and Pluralism

I am a frog
I live under a spell
I live at the bottom
Of a green well

And here I must wait
Until a maiden places me
On her royal pillow
And kisses me
In her father's palace.

The story is familiar
Everybody knows it well
But do other enchanted people feel as nervous
As I do? The stories do not tell,

Ask if they will be happier
When the changes come
As already they are fairly happy
In a frog's doom?

I have been a frog now
For a hundred years
And in all this time
I have not shed many tears,

I am happy, I like the life,
Can swim for many a mile
(When I have hopped to the river)
And am for ever agile.

And the quietness,
Yes, I like to be quiet

I am habituated
To a quiet life,

But always when I think these thoughts
As I sit in my well
Another thought comes to me and says:
It is part of the spell

To be happy
To work up contentment
To make much of being a frog
To fear disenchantment

Says, It will be *heavenly*
To be set free,
Cries, *Heavenly* the girl who disenchants
And the royal times, *heavenly*,
And I think it will be.

Come then, royal girl and royal times,
Come quickly,
I can be happy until you come
But I cannot be heavenly,
Only disenchanted people
Can be heavenly.

Stevie Smith, 'The Frog Prince'[1]

This poem is about transformation. The prefix trans- indicates change or movement. Transpose, transmute and transmit point beyond a static or paralysed present. Words like these work to encourage the fearful, frogs and others, to set aside the customary in favour of transformation and transcendence.

HILL VIEW COUNTY PRIMARY SCHOOL

Insoluble differences of religious and educational ideology

In 1987 Hill View Primary was difficult to find, as it consisted of one room and an office in a local community centre in the Asian area of the town. It was staffed by the Head and one temporary part-time teacher and had 30 infant pupils. The following academic year a couple of Portakabins were home to the staff of three and the 60 pupils recruited from the exclusively Muslim Asian families who lived in the terraces of Hill View. Damage caused by an arson attack delayed the school's normal operation until mid-October. Permanent buildings were under slow construction on land next to the community centre. Their completion would see the end to the bussing of Asian pupils from this area to schools scattered around the perimeter of the town. Bussing had been a cause of resentment and local political controversy. Consequently the new school was a political hot potato.

The Head had been appointed from a background in a multicultural education service and was concerned that the ethos of the school should win parental approval. He thought that RE had an important part to play in this and welcomed the development exercise as a forum for continual reflection on practice within the new school. From the outset, he saw home-school co-operation about the religious and moral development of pupils as a key to mutual trust and understanding in the turbulent racial, religious and political situation.

For reasons best known to the governors, he had little say in the appointment of the first two teachers. They expressed a general wish to have a 'balanced staff' having a range of expertise developed in different settings. Interviews led to the appointment of two women, a white teacher with experience in special needs and an Asian probationer. At first these teachers supported the work on an approach to home-school liaison, focusing on RE and school ethos.

> 'Having time to think things over as we go along may be a good thing. And [jokingly] we may be relieved to see a new face once we get sick of the sight of each other.'
>
> *(Fieldnote)*

A contributory factor in undertaking this work was the Head's own experience of religious faith as formative in shaping personal identity and lifestyle. He was an active member of the Church of England, involved in youth work, and thought it important that parents and children see their own Muslim religious tradition and values presented positively in school. On the basis of successful co-operation on sensitive religious matters, he hoped to involve parents in other aspects of their children's education.

The other staff had little experience of RE and had not considered it a crucial element of school life.

> 'I've never done much RE teaching before. It will be interesting to find out more about it. As all of the children go to mosque school, religion is something that I'm aware of here.'
>
> *(Fieldnote)*

> 'I suppose I must have done something on RE at college but I can't remember it. I have never taught it and lack confidence in it.'
>
> *(Fieldnote)*

There was a vast gap between the Head's plan for school RE development and staff competence and commitment to work with its religious dimension. The extent of this gulf emerged in discussions following the decision to work together on Ramadan, with a view to developing a programme of class-room work and school policies on issues which the festival raised: fasting, pupils' disrupted sleep patterns, excitement as Eid approached, declaring dates for the holiday. Sessions on this distinctively Muslim subject exposed disagreements over pupils' expression of a religious identity and the appropriateness of faith expression at all in a county maintained school.

The raised sensitivities were aggravated by media attention to Muslim fundamentalism as a political force. Muslim demands for voluntary aided schools also worried the staff. Their anxiety surfaced as a Flight from the RE work in school. Meetings started late and staff members did other things, such as cutting and mounting pupils' work as the meetings proceeded. Discussions were desultory and tasks set for completion for the next meeting were rarely completed. When the consultant interpreted this behaviour pattern as Flight from their fear of religion and RE, the women became angry, dismissing the work as valueless.

'With this Ramadan exercise we bit off more than we could chew. We should have started with something we felt more comfortable with.'

(Fieldnote)

'When I think of the real educational needs of these children, I get angry that we are spending time on this. As far as I'm concerned, it's like moving the deck chairs on the Titanic.'

(Fieldnote)

Staff talked of urgent curriculum needs in Science and Language in terms that sidelined the RE initiative.

'I've had an advisory teacher in my class doing the RE with me for five weeks, but I still don't feel any further forward. If I was going to have such intensive help, I'd rather have it in a core curriculum area.'

(Fieldnote)

The Flight behaviour changed direction and they geared up for a fight with the Head, whom they identified as the author of their RE discomfort. The time and space of the development exercise was being used by the participants as an arena for organizational nit-picking and professional disputes about literacy.

Media attention to Muslim culture, religion and educational aspirations in the wake of the Rushdie affair had made the staff nervous in their professional roles. The furore over Salman Rushdie's book *The Satanic Verses* erupted in a book burning in February 1989, which involved parents of some of the pupils. At national, local and institutional level it was clear that religion was political dynamite.

One of the teachers talked about the place of religion in her upbringing.

'When my father came to this country he removed his turban and shaved his beard. He wasn't really religious and he knew he would not get on in this country like that. I know I wear trousers all the time, but that's culture not religion. It's good to respect culture but the Salman Rushdie business shows religion can cause trouble.'

(Fieldnote)

'I'm really worried that all this religion talk will turn us into "a Muslim school". A lot of people around here already call us that. It isn't "a Muslim school". This religious thing is just the Head's concern; we don't support it. It's dangerous.'

(Fieldnote)

But continued publicity confirmed the Head's desire to work at these issues with openness and thought.

'We can't pretend that religion is not a real issue here. It's people in our situation who have to think it through.'

(Fieldnote)

There was a suspension of work at this point as the Head's ill health and the teachers' attendance at courses made after-school meetings impossible. Oddly enough the staff did not dispense with the consultancy. It was undeniably painful, but it appeared as if the trio could not feel safe together unless a consultant was present to prevent open hostilities.

When the sessions were resumed, there was a general recognition of the legal obligation to include RE in the curriculum. Staff decided to work on first principles and design
an RE curriculum policy for the school. Behind the new focus lay a desire to achieve
some shared norms and values to hold the group together. There was a fantasy that a
Pairing of the Head and the consultant as external saviour would produce a future
action plan that would satisfy everyone. This short-lived idyll was disrupted by a confrontation with their own anti-religious tendencies.

In late September the Head was ill. The remaining Hill View staff saw a video, *Islam
Through the Eyes of a Child*. As the programme proceeded they commented dis-
paragingly on the Muslim practices and lifestyles depicted. In discussion, they reviewed
their reactions to the film.

> 'It makes me angry to hear all that anti-feminist religious regulation stuff coming out of the mouths of
> young girls. At least all that bending, stretching and washing will ensure that they are fit and clean.'
>
> *(Fieldnote)*
>
> 'These kids have enough obstacles to face, what with language difficulties and racism, without the
> addition of religion.'
>
> *(Fieldnote)*

These exchanges began the dawn awareness of their own religious assumptions and
presuppositions. Gordon Lawrence identifies such moments as 'epiphanic' and describes
them in enticing terms as

> a discovery of an internal space where one has never explored . . . being able to put together
> feelings in a new way, for example something of one's personal history and the present. It
> is a moment of internal making and is purely of feeling. It is the nearest I have come to
> what I understand to be an epiphany, i.e. any moment of great or sudden revelation.[2]

It was poignant that on this occasion the feelings were of regret and embarrassment as
they realized the depth of their negativity towards their pupils' Muslim faith and beliefs.
The moment when the purveyors and tutors of courses on racial prejudice recognized
their own religious bias signalled the effective conclusion of RE curriculum work,
though the group continued to meet from time to time. The teachers needed time to
come to terms with the insight.

An event the following November enabled them to handle their feelings through
transference. Their pupils had been invited to a pantomime at a local Church of England
school. During an intermission, a white child was said to have made racist remarks to
some of the Hill View pupils. This was used to support the view that religious beliefs
lead to racism. The teachers refused to have any further contact with the school until
the staff had gone through a Racism Awareness Programme.

There was a lot of energetic discussion of racial prejudice in the area. The consultancy space was increasingly used to express anti-religious sentiments. The cause of
religion was firmly seen as 'the Head's thing'. To question the adequacies of religion was
a coded way of criticizing his leadership. Deterioration of the headmaster's health
caused him to seek employment outside primary education. A year later the older
teacher also left the school. Only one of the original staff moved into the completed
building.

ROLE, IDENTITY AND THE SCHOOL

The clarification of professional roles and organizational identity eats up a lot of energy at the foundation of a new enterprise. In a school, the enunciation of the teacher role defines the structured learning opportunities of pupils. The emergent identity of the school determines its recruitment, public profile, and the nature and quality of its external relations. Role conflict makes staff schizophrenic: identity conflict destroys the organization. The Hill View staff had to contend with both of these contra-indications of organizational health.

In *The Mikado*, Pooh Bah provides the archetype of role conflict when he is asked to advise on the financing of Ko-Ko's wedding.

> Of course, as First Lord of the Treasury, I could propose a special vote that would cover all expenses, if it were not that, as Leader of the Opposition, it would be my duty to resist it, tooth and nail. Or, as Paymaster-General, I could so cook the accounts that, as Lord High Auditor, I should never discover the fraud. But then, as Archbishop of Titipu, it would be my duty to denounce my dishonesty and give myself into my own custody as First Commissioner of Police.[3]

Like Pooh Bah, the teachers in this school saw themselves in an awkward situation, one set of commitments contra-indicating another. If they worked positively with the pupils' religious traditions, were they confirming the gender and authority stereotypes they actively critiqued in other aspects of their educational practice. If they ignored religion, they were in breach of the Education Reform Act 1988.

Creating an RE role for themselves was difficult for the women because of their antithetical stance towards religion. The Head, in contrast, could see the RE dimension of the curriculum as a focal point for the school.

> The self comes down to us from its own past. It needs and is a history. Each of us can see that his own idea of himself as this person is inseparably bound up with his view of his former life, of the plans that he formed, of the fortunes that fashioned him, and of the accomplishments which in turn he has fashioned for himself.[4]

Starting from radically opposed commitments, both of which claimed the moral high ground of justice and equality, the Head and his staff had been set on a collision course from the beginning.

The future of the school might have been brighter had he been able to propose his vision of the school, and the teachers' work towards that, at the interviews. If the Head and governors had shared preparation of a school mission statement, they could have recruited staff to support that vision. As it happened, the governors' belief that 'balanced staffing' would lead to balanced educational debate did not work well in practice.

This school serves as a good example of how identity is developed in interaction. It did not matter, at one level, how the staff wanted to see the school. To the people of the locality, who saw a playground full of Asian children, it was 'the Muslim school'. Staff were afraid that this nickname suggested that its educational approach was similar to that in Yusuf Islam's Islamia School in Brent, a 'Muslim school' with confessional aims which was going to apply for voluntary aided status. The locals' reference to 'the Muslim school' did not refer to educational methods or values but pin-pointed the unique situation of a school whose catchment area was inhabited by Muslim Asian families. The local designation suggested that the Head was onto something in his plan to tackle the religious issue in a positive way. But the inability of other staff to see religion as a positive value made failure and discord inevitable.

> It is only by virtue of internalization of institutionalized value that a genuine motivational integration of behaviour in the social structure takes place, that the 'deeper' layers of motivation become harnessed to the fulfilment of role expectations. It is only when this has taken place to a high degree that it is possible to say that a social system is highly integrated and the interests of the collective and the private interests of its constituent members can be said to approach coincidence.[5]

The seeds of Hill View's destruction were sown at the interviews. The appointments pulled together multicultural expertise, language and anti-racist specialisms with an ethnic minority staff member. Politically, the mix was perfect. However, the people didn't blend or share a common vision. The strength of their personal and professional convictions and experience sentenced the staff to permanent internal feuds, when their best individual intentions were to fight against racism and prejudice in the town and wider society. Charles Sorenson has said:

> It isn't the incompetent who destroy an organisation. The incompetent never get in a position to destroy it. It is those who have achieved something and want to rest upon their achievements who are forever clogging things up.[6]

Perhaps similar remarks could be made about those with tightly framed value positions. However, was it realistic to expect that three people in a small school in a small town could cope with differences and find solutions to educational, racial and religious problems that startle government and the wider society?

In the next story of development work, the staff of a Catholic school have to grapple with their different readings of a shared denominational tradition.

ST CLARE'S RC PRIMARY SCHOOL

Dealing with intra-denominational differences over RE development

St Clare's School is pleasantly situated in the suburbs of a seaside town and draws its pupils from two parishes. It has playing-field and playground space, and provides flexibly designed accommodation built in the late 1960s. The school has an annexe, St Catherine's, two miles away, which is housed in cramped, post-war temporary accommodation that has become disappointingly permanent. Administratively, these two units constitute one school, though the headteacher's office is on the St Clare's site and the bulk of his time is spent there. Both school and annexe have pupils across the whole age range. There are thirteen staff, with 243 pupils on the St Clare's site and 187 pupils at the St Catherine's annexe.

The Head was recently appointed and encouraged extensive curriculum development in the school. He was interested in everyone taking part in a long-term staff development exercise, committed to reflection on practice and thought, that would have more edge with external facilitation. RE had not been scrutinized for a number of years, though all the staff agreed that this subject was a priority in any Catholic school. There was clear interest in the subject, evidenced by the attendance of two staff members on a diocesan RE course which met one night a week over a two-year period. The RE work commenced amid a chorus of voices surprised that this important area had been ignored for so long.

Anecdotes of personal religious and RE history were a feature of the early meetings. The staff recalled experiences which accounted for their differing opinions and attitudes.

> 'In the 1940s and 1950s life seemed to be mapped out for you by the catechism. There were right answers to every question. It was a source of God-given advice and authority that was reinforced at home.'
>
> *(Fieldnote)*

> 'I was at school in the 1970s and 1980s and some of the rules and regulations you are talking about I'd never heard of till today. I don't remember much RE after primary school.'
>
> *(Fieldnote)*

> 'When I was a girl you knew where you stood with rules and morals. Now young people do not have the guidance which gave us our values, and family life is suffering.'
>
> *(Fieldnote)*

The group used contributions such as these to divide itself in two. One group were laughingly called 'The Vatican Oners' and the other 'The Vatican Twoers', recalling the revolutionary changes inaugurated in the Catholic Church in the 1960s by the Second Vatican Council.

The significance of the split was drawn to the consultant's attention by friction about the desirability of holding meetings on the St Catherine's site on some occasions. Those who had been identified as 'Oners', 'the old guard', were predominantly the staff at St Catherine's. The consultant offered the interpretation that staff were using the exercise to assert some essential difference between the groups on the two sites. This notion was supported by information that the LEA was dealing with a proposal to make the annexe a separate and expanded school in response to the rising population of St Catherine's parish. It was as if the staff was dangerously and pre-emptively seeking separate identities for the two schools.

> What has happened here will do
> To bite the living world in two,
> Half for me and half for you.
> Here at last I fix a line
> Severing the world's design
> Too small to hold both yours and mine.
> There's enormity in a hair
> Enough to lead men not to share
> Narrow confines of a sphere
> But put an ocean or a fence
> Between two opposite intents.
>
> *Adrienne Rich, 'Boundary'*[7]

This primitive division was only one way of defining and describing the ambiguous reality of their current religious experience. Discussions gave evidence of a widespread nostalgia for remembered security running alongside worries that received certainties were no longer consistent with the complexities and pressures of modern life.

'It's as if the picture of the world I was given no longer explains things and I have to reinvent the world. I feel betrayed and I'm not sure now what it is important to hand on.'

(Fieldnote)

'In college in the 1970s you didn't go to the Catholic Teachers' Certificate course to learn about RE, you went to get a passport to employment. So when I got into school I suppose I could only repeat what I had in primary school, with a few frills added to make it look more modern.'

(Fieldnote)

The group oscillated between Dependency and Fight behaviours, expressing their insecurities and fantasizing a dichotomy in the staff group. This relieved them of the burden of investigating their common experience of having ambivalent feelings about religious teaching. They were very confused.

> O I wish I could laugh! O I wish I could cry!
> Or find some formula, some mystical patter
> That would organize a perspective from this hellish scatter –
> Everywhere I look a part of me is exiled from the I.
>
> *Patrick Kavanagh, 'Nineteen Fifty-Four'*[8]

Since there appeared no dependable ecclesial authority which could reconcile these tensions, the group sundered its experience; staff on each site opting to live in the clarity of a half-truth which was inevitably a lie. When this position of problematic comfort had been negotiated, the staff decided cease meeting as a total group.

'I can't see that we are getting anywhere. I'm fed up and the consultant's no help. We haven't got time to stay with the ambivalences. We need answers. I'm a Catholic; I was brought up on answers. Maybe a small working group would be the answer.'

(Fieldnote)

This working group was a marriage of convenience which produced no saving consensus. During this phase, staff not involved in the group elaborated their assumptions about 'The Oners' and 'The Twoers' into exaggerated caricatures of the two parishes, which gave the impression that St Catherine's was a throw-back to the 1950s whilst St Clare's was in the vanguard of British Catholicism. Consequently, the annexe group were lobbying their RE representative for a curriculum based on catechism categories and doctrine, while the St Clare's faction pressured their nominee for an exploration of the ideas and philosophy behind the current National Catholic RE Project. The working party was trapped into a 'stand-off', only broken when the group met again to examine their fruitless labours.

The behaviour of the whole group was challenged by the Deputy Head.

'This is as ridiculous as the war in *Gulliver's Travels*, between those who open their eggs at the little end and those who open them at the big end. They were all keen on eggs and we're all concerned to get the RE right. But we can't work at it in case we suggest things that offend parents, priests or each other. We wouldn't be like this about any other subject.'

(Fieldnote)

She went on to describe some work her own class was doing on the Hindu festival of Divali, based on TV programmes for use in English lessons.

> 'It's going very well and the children need to know about the beliefs and cultures of other people in this country. I'm happy doing this but think it odd that it would not be acceptable in RE.'
>
> *(Fieldnote)*

These contributions, which brought together feeling and thought about practice, led the others to examine the constraints they believed Catholic orthodoxy imposed on pupils' religious education. Fears were expressed about the presentation of non-Christian traditions and the difficulty of presenting traditional teachings about marriage and family to those from single-parent families. In addition, they were struggling to recognize religious faith as a developing process rather than a static deposit of truth, to be able to build on the past rather than be determined by it. People talked about the cost of this in an ironic way.

> 'It takes so long. You either have to wait for some bit of you to die, or other people actually to die before the old ideas lose power.'
>
> *(Fieldnote)*

When one of their number announced formal withdrawal from further participation in the work, they had first-hand experience of the pain and loss this involves.

> 'I'm going to shut up for now on. Maybe I'm like the dodo, with my concern for truth and authority. Everyone will make more progress if I stop going on about doctrine and concentrate on Maths and Science.'
>
> *(Fieldnote)*

Whether this was blackmail, *hara-kiri* or assassination was not explored. Enthusiasm for renewal of the tradition had united the remaining staff to pursue narrative as a component in RE.

Some of them had read *Our Faith Story*[9], a publication of the National Catholic RE project and had found its proposal for a correlation between personal faith, autobiography and narratives of the Christian tradition very appealing. Work on a narrative approach to RE would be useful preparation for the introduction of the National Catholic RE programme in the early 1990s.

Two years after this work began formal notice of the rebuilding of St Catherine's School was posted on the door of St Clare's. By the time that new buildings were completed, both schools would be using the same national RE scheme.

BRINGING THE NEW INTO BEING

If everything remains the same, there's no reason to change. Growth and development happen when there is some element of tension in a situation. If the tension between people is minimal, there will be no stimulus to action. If the air is electric with the tension produced by rival ambitions or beliefs, no talk or work is possible. The ideal for useful exchange is enough tension to stimulate without inducing unbearable strain. It could be described as the Goldilocks principle of development: 'not too much, not too little, but something just right'.

Life at St Clare's with St Catherine's had its share of tension, enough to make things interesting without being too scarey. Throughout the disagreement over RE, birthdays were celebrated, liturgical occasions observed and photographs of school trips continued to cause good-humoured banter.

The expression of counter-dependent aggression towards the consultant and the progress of the work came from a sense of betrayal, which went beyond this curriculum exercise. The staff shared a fantasy of some cataclysmic moment in the 1960s which held dislocated history, dividing an era of paradisal order from the present post-lapsarian value distress. They had no conceptual way of bridging the gulf between their own religious autobiographies and the stories and doctrines which expressed Church identity. Consequently, they felt like children abandoned in a wood by wicked parents.

The existence and relevance of *Our Faith Story* offered them a reliable and authoritative framework for using biblical narrative to speak to the present Catholic identity crisis. Working in this way released the totality of their ambiguous experience as a resource.

> 'I've always thought, "I've got ideas, things have happened to me." But they're separate from religion – secular, worldly. Now I'm excited. Instead of playing with half a pack of cards, I can use the full deck.'
>
> *(Fieldnote)*

When the group had established a secure and shared basis for work, they could draw on all the resources of their common tradition.

> In any cultural field it is not possible to be original except on a basis of tradition. Conversely, no one in the line of cultural contributors repeats except as a deliberate quotation, and the unforgiveable sin in the cultural field is plagiarism. The interplay between originality and the acceptance of tradition as the basis for inventiveness seems to be just one more example, and a very exciting one, of the interplay between separateness and union.[10]

The rediscovery of the classic texts of Christianity and the capacity to hear them differently in a 1980's context meant that the staff had new stories to tell and live out towards a transformed future.

THE NARRATIVE QUALITY OF EXPERIENCE

In 1971 Stephen Crites observed that 'the formal quality of experience through time is essentially narrative'[11]. The telling of stories is the only way to articulate the intentionality of human activity. Picking out a thread or plot in the endless stream of life events and happenings is a way of celebrating the purposeful and successful undertakings which drive history forward. It turns mere events and happenings into experience.

Crites' article concentrated on the relation between biblical narrative and human experience. He highlighted 'the sacred story, the mundane story and the temporal form of experience itself: three narrative tracks, each constantly reflecting and affecting the course of the others'.[12] This is the narrative dialogue which excited staff at St Clare's and St Catherine's, enabling them to move beyond the tenacious recitation of their contending narratives of conviction. But the ability to tell these stories was all important. However unsatisfactory these narratives were, they bound together people and life events into an intelligible and interpreted pattern which described how and explained why they had arrived at their current personal and professional stances.

In other schools too, the autobiographical element was essential to staff dialogue. The dynamic of the RE work in each school was the movement from 'my story' to 'our story', from narratives of individualism to a narrative which gave form to curriculum values held in common. To share this process and progress with others it was necessary to write the eight school stories which appear in this book, as an attempt to interpret and make intelligible the muddle of things said, done, read and avoided over a two-year period in the pursuit of improved practice. As Crites pointed out: 'Only narrative form can contain the tensions, the surprises, the disappointments and reversals and achievements of actual temporal experience'.[13] In secular discourse people rarely row over the historicity of events. However, traitors and martyrs are those who apply hermeneutical perspectives which others consider illegitimate to traditional readings of history or religious stories. Salman Rushdie is the most recent *cause célèbre*. The question of who owns a story, who has authority to determine its meaning and express the limits of its application, is a live issue for RE teachers as well as those accused of blasphemy. In *Haroun and the Sea of Stories*, Rushdie describes the origin of narratives, 'the Ocean of the Streams of Story', as home to the infinitely mutable.

> And because the stories were held here in fluid form, they retained the ability to change, to become new versions of themselves, to join up with other stories and so become yet other stories; so that unlike a library of books, the Ocean of the Streams of Story was much more than a store-room of yarns. It was not dead but alive.[14]

The wholly novel story or idea emerges from establishing new connections between elements of existing experience. The 'entirely new' is only so in comparison with its immediate forerunner.

THE PATTERN WHICH CONNECTS[15]

Gregory Bateson was concerned with the relationships and connections between elements of experience. He talked about this in terms of the 'forms', the 'patterns' which connected them, and the new 'order' which the relationships created. Speaking to Rollo May, he referred to these patterns as 'old friends'.

> . . . these patterns which I have met with before
> And shall meet again
> And which tell me that things are alive . . .
> These patterns exist in the morphogenesis
> of marigolds
> They exist in the morphogenesis of forests
> They exist in the book I am trying to write
> And in any debate among clusters of people.
> They are the necessary outward and visible sign
> Of the system being organised . . .[16]

Bateson's pattern, translated into existential terms, has much in common with myth, a narrative structure which gives pattern and order to human history. Like pattern, the

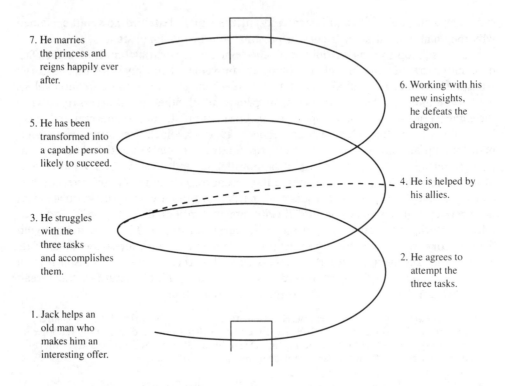

7. He marries the princess and reigns happily ever after.

5. He has been transformed into a capable person likely to succeed.

3. He struggles with the three tasks and accomplishes them.

1. Jack helps an old man who makes him an interesting offer.

6. Working with his new insights, he defeats the dragon.

4. He is helped by his allies.

2. He agrees to attempt the three tasks.

Figure 3 *The story of Foolish Jack*

myth is not a datum of human experience, but something invented after the fact, to throw light on structural similarities which are only apparent after the passage of time and events. The myth is created by editing the formless, meaningless material to focus on an essential pattern inherent in life's data. The pattern, the story, the myth, reveals itself as the product of a reflective process which seeks to make connections. Joseph Campbell describes the general pattern of myth in *The Hero with a Thousand Faces*:

> A hero ventures forth from the world of the common day into a region of supernatural wonder: fabulous forces are there encountered and a decisive victory is won: the hero comes back from this with the power to bestow boons on his fellow man.[17]

It is a quest undertaken to possess a power which can transform the lives of others. CREATE's work in school had something of this dynamic. But whilst Campbell's 'heroic journey' marked the stages of the individual's internal quest for integration and wholeness, the pattern inherent in the school work was more akin to the external quest described in fairy-tales, which are undertaken for personal and social transformation.

All of the school participants started off entranced by a future vision of themselves as competent and skilled working teams, able to renew their RE curriculum practice. All had to come to terms with the changes needed in themselves to accomplish that objective. Project participation was not the miraculous gift of three wishes granted, but a painful commitment to professional growth. Nor was this a simple linear development. It was a wheeling, spiral movement towards an evolving future which turned around the axis of the given social setting of each school. It involved the sacrifice of inadequate perceptions and substantial catharsis on the part of all involved. To travel this route was to rename aspects of reality, consent to growth and change, and to act on new perceptions.

This process is more colourfully recapitulated in fairy-stories such as *Foolish Jack*, modelled on the spiral in Figure 3.

In this tale, the woodcutter's third and silly son meets an old man whose beard is caught in a tree. When Jack frees him, he is asked if he would like to kill the dragon, marry the princess and become the king of the country.

Jack is eager for the prize, but he must do the old man a favour by rerouting the river which floods his cave. Then he will receive the magic sword 'Dragon-slayer'.

He is helped by obliging beavers who build a dam and change the river's course. Armed with Dragon-slayer he now has to find the dragon and work out how to get close enough to use the sword. He tricks the evil witch out of her cloak, 'Invisible', and is led to the dragon's lair by birds he frees from the fowler's net.

Jack has come through many tests and trials and discovered his own untapped resources of courage and skill. By the time he defeats the dragon he is every inch the mature hero and a princess's natural consort.

Now he is the wise and compassionate ruler who will lead his citizens into the 'happy ever after'.

In any fairy-tale the offer of gifts features early in the story and the victory, marriage and coronation are dealt with rather tersely. The narrative art is lavished on the struggle for transformation and the surmounting of obstacles. Like professional development and curriculum development in school, the real action and learning is in this process rather than the accomplished goal.

STORY AND PROFESSIONAL DEVELOPMENT

Since this kind of work is as risky as Goldilocks' walk in the woods, one would like to think that the effects of one stroll would last a lifetime. CREATE's excursion in active reflection suggests that societal and educational changes will require school staffs to co-operate in repeated woodland meanderings.

> So
> Into the woods you go again
> You have to every now and then.
> Into the woods, no telling when,
> Be ready for the journey.
>
> Into the woods, but not too fast
> Or what you wish you lose at last.
> Into the woods, but mind the past.
> Into the woods, but mind the future. . . .
>
> The way is dark,
> The light is dim,
> But now there's you,
> Me, her and him.
> The chances look small,
> The choices look grim,
> But everything you learn there

Will help when you return there.

The light is getting dimmer . . .

I think I see a glimmer –

Into the woods – you have to grope,
But that's the way you learn to cope.
Into the woods to find there's hope
Of getting through the journey.

Into the woods, each time you go,
There's more to learn of what you know.
Into the woods, but not too slow –
. . .

Into the woods,
Into the woods,
Then out of the woods –
And happy ever after!

I wish . . .

Stephen Sondheim, 'Into the Woods'[18]

NOTES AND REFERENCES

1. *The Frog Prince and Other Poems* (1966) (London: Longman), pp. 1–2.
2. G. Lawrence (1985) 'Beyond the frames', in M. Pines (ed), *Bion and Group Psychotherapy* (London: Routledge & Kegan Paul), p. 327.
3. W. S. Gilbert, *The Mikado*.
4. J. Royce (1968) *The Problem of Christianity*, (Chicago: Henry Regnery), Vol 12. p. 40.
5. T. Parsons (1951) *The Social System* (New York: Free Press), p. 42.
6. Charles Sorenson, quoted in R. B. White (ed.) (1988) *The Last Word in Management* (London: Foulsham), p. 294.
7. *Poems Selected and New 1950–1974* (1975) (New York: W. W. Norton), p. 5.
8. *Collected Poems* (1972) (London: Martin Brian & O'Keefe), p. 147.
9. A. P. Purnell (1985) *Our Faith Story: Its Telling and Its Sharing* (London: Collins Liturgical).
10. R. Fulton (1971) *The Spaces between the Stories* (New York: New Rivers Press), p. 99.
11. S. Crites (1971) 'The narrative quality of experience', *Journal of the American Academy of Religion*, **39**(3), 291–311.
12. *Ibid*, p. 305.
13. *Ibid*, p. 306.
14. S. Rushdie (1990) *Haroun and the Sea of Stories* (London: Granta Books), p. 72.
15. A phrase used by Bateson to describe 'nature's metaphors', structural similarity or similarity in the organization of dynamic reality. The argument in this section depends heavily on his work: G. Bateson (1972) *Steps to an Ecology of Mind* (New York: Ballantine); (1979) *Mind and Nature* (New York: Dutton).
16. R. May (1978) 'Gregory Bateson and humanistic psychology', in J. Brockman (ed.), *About Bateson* (London: Wildwood), pp. 85–6.
17. J. Campbell (1949) *The Hero with a Thousand Faces* (New York: Pantheon Books), p. 30.
18. *Into the Woods* (1989) (New York: Theatre Communications Group), pp. 137–8.

Part Four

Future Possibilities

Chapter 10 specifies the difficulties and the potential areas of development in whole-school RE work. Ten principles are offered as a guide to policy-making and curriculum planning. Chapter 11 is a closing reflection on the crucial contribution of RE to understanding and handling conflicts of commitment.

Chapter 10

Landmarks in Learning

Don't think of magic as a conjuring trick
Or just as fortune-tellers reading hands.
It is a secret which will sometimes break
Through ordinary days, and it depends

Upon right states of mind like good intent,
A love that's kind, a wisdom that is not
Pleased with itself. This sort of magic's meant
To cast a brilliance on dark trains of thought

To guide you through the mazes of the lost,
Lost love, lost people and lost animals.
For this, a sure, deep spell of care is cast

Which never lies and will not play you false.
It banishes the troubles of the past
And is the oldest way of casting spells.

Elizabeth Jennings, 'Considering Magic'[1]

Curriculum development is not the preserve of magicians who produce happiness with a wave of the wand. Progress towards transformed practice depends on illuminating the turbulent, dispossessed and fearful aspects of human beings. George Eliot speaks of these in terms of 'a great deal of unmapped country within us which would have to be taken into account in an explanation of our gusts and storms'.[2] This mysterious psychological territory is not easily apparent and there are no tricks to undermine its power. It requires a quality of care and a wisdom manifest in the will to maintain a search for understanding. Such efforts are powered by a compassion for human confusion and lostness that should be a feature of any curriculum or group relations consultancy.

One can understand the desire not to be overwhelmed by mystery, especially one's own. In the educational maze the magical and practical guide would be one who adopts a surveyor role, highlighting landmarks and erecting signposts to aid the hapless traveller. Any wanderer who sought direction could then find clear warnings of problems and clear indications of the best ways forward. The school-based research work described in this book offers pointers to problematic and potential development areas of RE curriculum work.

POINTERS TO THE PROBLEMS

One is invariably grateful for the identification of a path better avoided, clearly named as likely to cause grief. However, the pointers described in this section demand a different response. They direct attention to difficult aspects of school life and behaviour which require visitation in the course of RE curriculum development work if any conclusions are to address the real situation. They indicate 'the road less travelled but which will "make all the difference".'

Whilst acknowledging that these routes have their assault course connotations, these pointers are offered to indicate fruitful directions which emerged from the consultancies in the project schools. Others, experiencing similar dynamics, may find the pointers useful in exploration of these areas of group life, illuminating and identifying unconscious, relational and political factors which affect R.E. work in their own situations. Since the 'pointers' emerged from particular school settings, they are presented in context.

George Street

Oscillation between Dependent and counter-Dependent behaviour was a feature of work here. So long as staff relied totally on the Head, an outside expert or imported solutions for their difficulties, they avoided responsibility for their own actions or inactivity. They were doomed to paralysis until they critiqued their own blaming of others and adherence to rigid hierarchical patterns. While they waited for the new bit of information from the outside expert or the 'correct' direction from the Head, their own competence and trust in each other shrivelled. When this was apparent, self-directed and co-operative learning could be explored.

Michael Rossman enthuses about self-directed learning.

> The learner . . . learns as much by the process of his own creation as by recreating others' past learning . . . His learning in a subject takes him deep in its penetration of his self, and outward in its embodiment in society. He grows along his subject as a vine does along a trellis, over many years and windings.[3]

This gentle development in George Street was characterized by many small rays of insight, which were assimilated over a long period rather than one piercing ray of enlightenment which gave the 'whole truth'. However, the gradualness allowed the dawning recognition that the roots of their attitudes to RE teaching lay in their inability to deal with their own diversity. Their denial of variety in the school staff and wider society had led them to regard any expressed religious interests or practice as a disqualification from RE teaching.

C of E (withdrew)

The withdrawal of this small school indicates that there are good times and bad times for development work. The appointment of an external candidate as deputy head led to a redundancy on the staff. A second member of staff stated her intention to resign. In the light of this unforeseen staffing upheaval, the school decided not to continue work on RE development. Rapid and unexpected turnover in staff is a strong contra-indication for work of this sort. Provisionality and insecurity are unstable foundations for risky activity.

St Benedict's RC

Emotion ran high in this school. Changes in admissions policy and worries about the school's survival, as it no longer served a majority Catholic intake, generated insecurity tinged with belligerence. All the pressures tended to push for political action to secure a future within the diocesan structures. But this did not meet the staff's need for reassurance about the place of their school under the umbrella of Catholic educational tradition. Poets and analysts point out:

> Becoming absorbed in the one-dimensional current of instant speech we are in danger of losing both the will and ability to attend to echoes. Still less are we ready to wait on what lies beyond them.[4]

The presenting hunger for action in St Benedict's was overriding a need to reconstrue old loyalties in new situations. This was the source of staff passions and anxiety. The group needed to process their ambiguous feelings so that they could encounter unfamiliar and emergent attitudes, the 'as-yet-pathless' in themselves. This work enabled them to reach a greater degree of attunement to their inner psychological worlds and the external context. They also discovered the courage and creativity appropriate to their RE task. Though it was uncomfortable, it was essential to sift the turbulent feelings of the staff, so that they could reconceptualize RE beyond the catechetical mode.

Table 10.1   *Area A Schools*

	Pointers to the problems
George Street	Autocratic leadership style
	Reliance on the outside expert
	A belief in one right answer/one right way of doing things
	Projection
	Scapegoating
	Acting as if possession of personal faith should disqualify people from teaching RE
C of E (withdrew)	Unexpected school restructuring
	Sudden changes in staffing
St Benedict's RC	Significant change in the type of pupils recruited by the school
	Fears for the survival of the school
	Mistrust between the staff and governing body
	Idealization of the past
	Ambivalence
	Fear of change
	Acting as if the denominational nature of the school required an exclusive doctrinal approach to RE

Table 10.2   *Area B Schools*

	Pointers to the problems
Richmond Road	Concern to keep everyone happy Setting up a group to contain the anxiety of the larger organization Lack of a clear aim Lack of authority to influence or implement Loss of energy and enthusiasm Loss of personnel from the work Acting as if RE in school is to produce socially acceptable behaviour
Ryesdon C of E	Professional issues processed as if they were interpersonal problems No clarity about the role of staff member or RE teacher Work imposed on the staff by a departing Head Paralysis Fear of fragmenting the staff group Acting as if shared though unexamined religious assumptions hold the group together
St Clare's with St Catherine's RC	Caricature Fantasies about the attitudes and self-understanding of others Withdrawal Artificial internal divisions Presentation of an edited version of current experience Plans for future changes in school organization A belief that religious education occurs only under the discreet heading of RE Acting as if RE is about orthodoxy

Table 10.3   *Area C Schools*

	Pointers to the problems
Hill View	Ideological intransigence Desire that the school should sanction and sponsor personal values Insecurity about school identity Staff absence No shared 'mission' for the school which helps staff create roles Self-justification Transference Acting as if religious faith and belief is antithetical to education and justice
St Mark's C of E	Fear of 'the foreign' Suspicion Feelings of personal inadequacy in relation to religious knowledge, attitude and skills Fear of disunity Acting as if RE in schools keeps British culture British
St Peter's RC	Denial of the environment in which pupils live Suppression of difference/minority reports Difficulty in finding time to work on RE curriculum Silence Tension between personal life and professional expectations Compliance with coercion Strong external constraints Mourning for lost roles and status Acting as if RE should be kept 'safe' so that it should not attract adverse criticism from clergy or diocese

Richmond Road

In *The Mill on the Floss*, George Eliot describes human beings as embodying two distinct ways of being in the world. 'The men of maxims' are judged alongside 'the people of broad, strong sense' and are found wanting. Her sympathies lie with the latter.

> . . . such people early discern that the mysterious complexity of our life is not to be embraced by maxims, and that to lace ourselves up in formulas of that sort is to repress all the divine promptings and inspirations that spring from growing insight.[5] And the man of maxims is the popular representative of the minds that are guided in their moral judgement solely by general rules, thinking that these will lead them to justice by a ready-made patent method, without the trouble of exerting patience, discrimination, impartiality – without any care to assure themselves whether they have the insight that comes from a hardly-earned estimate of temptation, or from a life vivid and intense enough to have created a wide fellow-feeling with all that is human.[6]

These ways of being resonate with the experience of the Richmond Road staff and identify the dichotomy they had to explore before they could move on. Their reliance on practical procedures effectively blocked their efforts at renewal. They met their insecurity about what to do with a misplaced confidence that they knew precisely the method by which it would be achieved. Borne on this administrative tide, they pictured themselves as good curriculum managers: efficient, effective and economical with time. The sidelining of their proposals by colleagues called this self-image and their curriculum management stategies into question. The lack of clear aim, authority or influence and the loss of staff participation were clear indications that the work had run into difficulties. But working party members were blind to them all.

The RE task got lost in an eagerness to model good working party behaviours and structures for the rest of the staff. This was a novel way of enacting the assumption, widely voiced in the school, that anything to do with RE was to do with good behaviour. It was only towards the end of the consultation that working party members recognized the redundancy of procedure as an adequate strategy. In the last meeting there was a degree of self-questioning. Some suspected that their working style had been devised to avoid the painful divisions about religion and RE and regretted that they had not done more to understand this depth of feeling.

Rysedon C of E

Worry about the identity and future of the Church of England was a significant issue in this school. It bubbled up in factional jibes which ruffled surface assertions of togetherness and agreement.

Dissension in the Church signalled a corresponding crisis in school RE policy and practice. Any attempt to introduce new practice without addressing this religious insecurity would have been like trying to build on quicksand. Work on the programme in the school highlighted the variety of religious conviction and expression in the staff. Co-operation at any level was difficult when each was involved in apologia and the manufacture of personal defences.

The way to RE renewal had to take in an examination of the breadth of Church of England tradition and appreciate the staff group as representatives of it. But the teachers resisted opportunities for any type of learning which would surface and engage the faith commitment of individuals. This group called to mind Carlos Castenada's combative enquirers.

> A man goes to knowledge . . . as he goes to war, wide awake, with fear . . . He slowly begins to learn – bit by bit at first, then in big chunks. His thoughts so clash. What he learns is never what he pictured, or imagined, and so he begins to be afraid . . . Every step of learning is a new task, and the fear begins to mount . . . Fear! A terrible enemy – treacherous and difficult to overcome.[7]

The indicators of the end of purposeful RE work were the designation of learning as an enemy and the reluctance to test the religious assumptions thought to hold the group together.

St Clare's with St Catherine's RC

Introspection is just one strategy for attending to the fundamental difficulties of RE development. Consideration of events within the wider sphere, like plans for a new school, can also point to fruitful lines of enquiry.

The fact that St Clare's with St Catherine's was to become two separate institutions, gave an objective basis for interpreting references to internal divisions. The staff's preemptive attempts to split the school began the process of negotiating new organizational identities. The caricatured images they advanced, however, pointed towards a polarization of religious attitudes likely to cut across a coherent RE policy. Events in this school show how organizational change releases suppressed elements in a group. This encourages the tendency for staff to process their internal confusion in terms which mirror institutional events.

Alarm bells ought to ring at the sudden discovery that one territory has been occupied for years by two opposing factions. This is a strong indication that a group cannot integrate the ambiguities or variety within its own experience and is avoiding recognition of this by asserting simplistic dichotomies and exclusivities. Progress here was only possible when those involved had grasped the nettle of personal ambivalence towards their common denominational history and traditions. Only then could they discover that dialectical living can be both challenging and creative.

> We can talk, then, of living between the opposites. To live between means that we not only recognize opposites, but rejoice that they exist . . . To live between we stretch out our arms and push the opposites as far apart as we can, and then live in the resonating space between them . . . Rejoicing in the opposites means pushing the opposites apart with our imaginations so as to create space, and then enjoying the fantastic music coming from each side.[8]

Hill View

In Hill View there was no tradition or sense of school identity. The school had been established because of years of political wrangling between parents and the LEA about education and race. The contentious practice of bussing was brought to an end by opening Hill View, but the governors had failed to indicate a distinctive 'mission' for the school.

Their staff recruitment policy, based on criteria of breadth and balance of experience, succeeded in recruiting a Head and two teachers who had privately framed the 'mission' of the school in radically different terms. So the political furore over race, religion and education was bequeathed to the staff, turning all meetings into battlefields and effectively preventing common purpose in curriculum policy.

Since the staff had been selected as exemplars of anti-racist, non-prejudicial educational practice, they found it difficult to confront their own anti-religious assumptions. It was evident that some staff members understood their commitment to equal opportunites required a distancing from religious traditions, which saw the role of women, male authority and the purposes of education in terms very different from 1980s secularism. Their way to improved practice lay in questioning these presuppositions and exploring how these attitudes affected relationships and RE practice in the school. This involved traumatic disorganization and reorganization of previously denied perceptions which would need time and courage to work through.

St Mark's C of E

Like the teachers at Hill View, the staff here also had to proceed in a critical processing of their RE prejudices. This tested the comfortable working relations built up over years. Advancement was won at the risk of disunity.

An initial audit of the factors affecting school pupils had shown that the multiracial and multifaith nature of the town required development of the exclusively Christian RE curriculum. Staff resistance to change was strong, as many interpreted this as a prologue to the admittance of Asian pupils. The RE issue was then overwhelmed by catastrophic fears over the loss of coherence of race, religion, language, literacy and culture in the school. When it was clear that the school would continue to recruit white Christian pupils from its existing catchment area, the opposition to RE change shifted to focus on staff ignorance of world faith traditions. Whilst some were keen to expand their knowledge and curricular options, others approaching retirement or set in their ways complained that the change was an attack on British tradition and culture.

The staff was unable to decide on a definite policy until they were galvanized by the accusations of racism levied by the Hill View teachers. This enabled them to set aside self-interest and pull together, harnessing their varied resources towards an RE programme designed to promote equality and justice.

St Peter's RC

Progress in RE in this school depended upon taking action in a situation which denied staff the authority to act. Unable to engage in critical reflection on education or tap into contemporary Catholic resources, staff RE work consisted in developing appealing ways of presenting their 'orthodox' pre-Vatican II script.

Change depended upon the staff travelling down a questioning road, enquiring about the relation between religious tradition and life, and confronting the 'orthodoxies' about world faiths and paganism urged upon them out of the self-interest of others. This road was a hard one to travel, guarded by heavy authority positions, requiring a struggle to find words to name the experience of the 'anomalous faithful', those who find their attachment to Catholicism a little frayed. There were hints that some in the group thought that there might be a map to this difficult terrain. But they declined such a perilous trip and retreated into an unnerving silence which variously screamed dumb apathy, baffled confusion, impasse, muzzled outrage, reproachful censure, tacit approval, palpable menace, self-accusation and ultimately resignation.

* * *

This short review of the difficulties encountered *en route* to curriculum renewal presents the ironic view that potential for development lies in addressing the most problematic elements of current group experience.

This is not intended as a do-it-yourself approach to RE development. The turn about from problem to potential is only discerned because of the consultancy relationship which supports this type of work. In all of the schools described in this book, the consultant was contracted to facilitate beneficial change in RE practice and understood that staff would be at the same time enthusiastic and reluctant to make that change. This model of curriculum consultancy draws upon psychotherapy, concerned to affirm and accept the client whilst helping that client reject their dysfunctional aspects. What Carl Rogers says of therapeutic relationships is the key to transforming the problems into potential.

> This painful dis- and reorganization is made possible by two elements in the therapeutic relationship. The first is that the new, the tentative, the contradictory, or the previously denied perceptions of self are as much valued by the therapist as the rigidly structured aspects. Thus the shift from the latter to the former become possible without too frightening a leap from the old to the new. The other element in the relationship is the attitude of the therapist toward the newly discovered aspects of experience. To the client they seem threatening, bad, impossible, disorganizing. Yet he experiences the therapist's attitude of calm acceptance toward them. He finds that to a degree he can introject this attitude and can look upon his experience as something he can own, identify, symbolize, and accept as part of himself.[9]

POINTERS TO THE POSSIBILITIES

The transformation of problems into possibilities is an example of the quality of careful attention and intention which consultancy can generate (see Table 10.4 on p. 125).

George Street

The key insight which helped RE development in this school was the move towards a co-operative working style. This enabled everyone to value and direct their own particular abilities and resources into the production of an RE policy which had the support of all. The staff's positive experience of co-operative debate as professionally maturing led to a change in the management style of the school in general.

Table 10.4 *Pointers to the possibilities*

A	George Street	The adoption of a co-operative working style which values the commitments of each as a positive resource for group work
	C of E (withdrew)	
	St Benedict's RC	Setting aside time and human energy to explore staff feelings, assumptions and fears
B	Richmond Road	Understanding that the RE work was initially about staff development and policy rather than about the production of lesson plans
	Ryesdon C of E	Recognition of a dynamic and diverse denominational identity*
	St Clare's with St Catherine's RC	Imaginative engagement with the autobiographical aspects of RE work
C	Hill View	An exploration of attitudes influencing RE*
	St Mark's C of E	Preparedness to work together on an RE programme to challenge racial and religious prejudice
	St Peter's RC	Willingness to struggle with the ambiguities of Church history, so as to re-present religion as a resource for understanding contemporary issues*

*These 'pointers' were not fully realized in the school situations. They are offered here to indicate elements present in the situation which could be mobilized in future work.

St Benedict's RC

The staff in this school nicknamed the RE exercise 'Time and Space' as they came to value the work as an opportunity to explore the powerful commitments, fears and feelings aroused by the religious dimension of the school's life. They recognized that 'talk' was central to RE management and that opportunities for professional conversation had to be built into the timetable. Curriculum proposals which lacked this foundation would inevitably be weak in practice.

Richmond Road

The pressure to supply others with answers and lesson plans drove the efforts of this group into a cul-de-sac. But sometimes the right road is only discovered by realizing the redundancy of a wrong turn. Late in the day they recognized that more discussion and wider exchange about the role and purpose of RE would have served their enterprise better.

Ryesdon C of E

The Church of England describes itself as a broad national church. Had staff in Ryesdon been able to explore the implications of that for their own situation as a denominational foundation serving a locality, rather than a parish, they might have been freed from factional infighting. Then the RE discussions could have been framed as a school and pedagogical issue rather than a forum for the settling of interpersonal religious disputes.

St Clare's with St Catherine's RC

RE development is a creative venture and relies on the imagination. Staff in this school were empowered to work when they were able to appropriate the title of a book about RE in Catholic schools, *Our Faith Story*. This metaphor of RE as story-telling, understood in co-relation with the experience of their own spiritual journeys, enabled them to recognize that the larger religious story contained different moments and perspectives often at odds with each other. The enlargement of their religious imagination to appreciate the need for multifaith approaches emphasizes the roles of autobiography and creativity in development exercises of this sort.

Hill View

Adults make commitments and stick to them with integrity. The implications of these loyalties disclose themselves over the passage of time, often demanding a reinterpretation or relativization of the stance originally taken. This is the challenge which confronted Hill View's staff when they discovered their religious intolerance. An examination of their personal and professional attitudes was an essential first step in dealing with RE as an important curriculum area.

St Mark's C of E

The turning-point for staff at St Mark's came when their defences against new RE practice were penetrated by an accusation of sponsoring racist behaviour in their pupils. This charge contradicted the image they had of their school as a place fostering Christian values of kindness and love of neighbour. They worked together in an effort to move their compassionate aspirations into a living experience.

St Peter's RC

In the final analysis, people and institutions change if it is in their interests to do so. It is not advisable to introduce change that could bring criticism from sponsors or authority figures best kept as allies.

The staff at St Peter's had a 'safety-first' policy on RE because they pictured their diocesan employers as punitive and regressive. They had first-hand experience of change in the religious climate of the locality, but professional self-interest prevented the intrusion of 'recent and relevant' into RE. A full exploration of the non-fit between RE as taught and life as lived in town C awaits the day when 'the authorities' give it official sanction.

TEN PRINCIPLES FOR RE CURRICULUM DEVELOPMENT

The practical work in schools yielded much rich data which has been described and interpreted here. Out of that it is possible to distil ten principles which distinguish a consultancy-based RE development approach. (See Table 10.5 on page 127.)

1. Co-operative, collegial working styles generate a high degree of interest and loyalty in the work undertaken.

   The schools most successful in achieving policy statements and curriculum proposals were those whose staff groups could work together, having the courage to ask uncomfortable questions about the origins of existing curriculum rationale and practice. This is clearly evident in the work of George Street, St Benedict's and St Mark's. Conversely, the experience of Ryesdon and St Peter's suggest that an inability to work together offers a poor prognosis for development work.

   The skills of co-operative working must either be in place or develop on the back of RE curriculum work if it is to provide a safe environment for discussing controversial topics.

2. Development occurs when there is time and available energy for free-ranging and exploratory talk around the key issues.

   The experience of St Benedict's is the clearest example of this important principle. Unlike those at St Peter's, staff here had time to develop a shared professional language and talk themselves into shared policy and action. They embarked on the exercise at the same time as Richmond Road, but were not seduced into syllabus production at too early a stage. They had the advantage, unavailable to their peers in the large school, of staying together throughout the work. This made it easier for them to take ownership of the final outcomes of the work and see the benefits from the work in their broader professional life together. The data from George Street, St Clare's with St Catherine's and St Mark's also bears out this principle.

   In places such as St Peter's or Hill View, where time for talk together was short and talk itself 'unsafe', insights were painfully won and progress was slow.

3. Exploration of the feelings affecting the situation gives rise to new thoughts about it.

   This principle highlights the psychodynamic dimension of curriculum development. It recognizes that work may be overwhelmed by powerful anxieties and that human feeling gives rise to new thoughts. Progress at George Street, St Benedict's, St Clare's with St Catherine's and St Mark's witnesses to the utility of this principle. It was also relevant in enabling staff at St Peter's, Hill View and Richmond Road to identify and understand the assumptions and commitments which worked against improving RE practice in their schools at that time.

   > How, but by the medium of a world like this? . . . Do you not see how necessary a World of Pains and troubles is to school an Intelligence and make it a soul? A Place where the heart must feel and suffer in a thousand diverse ways! Not merely is the Heart a Hornbook, it is the Mind's Bible, it is the Mind's experience, it is the teat from which the mind or intelligence sucks its identity.[10]

4. Professional learning takes place when a staff group can stay with the
    experience of 'not knowing', resisting a rush to quick solutions.
        Chapter 3 referred to the primary teacher's concern that all questions
    have answers, making the observation that this attitude rang the death
    knell of adult professional learning. This principle endorses the danger
    in this position. 'Our ignorance with all the intermediates of obscurity
    is the *condition* of our ever increasing knowledge'.[11] The RE initiative in
    Richmond Road foundered on the shoals of the staff's confidence in the
    power of procedure and administration. There was widespread enthusiasm
    in project schools for pre-emptive goal setting and practical activity before
    issues had been thought through. The case studies supply many examples
    of where talk and reflective and theoretical work was dismissed as a waste
    of time.
        The challenge in RE development is to see things afresh and suspend the
    memory of the previously known.

    > By listening to what is being said and by watching ourselves a little bit, we learn some-
    > thing, we experience something; and from that learning and experiencing we look.
    > [But] we look with the memory of what we have learned and with what we have
    > experienced; with that memory in mind we look. Therefore it is not looking, it is not
    > learning. Learning implies a mind that learns each time anew. So it is always fresh to
    > learn. Bearing that in mind we are not concerned with the cultivation of memory but
    > rather to observe and see what actually takes place. We will try to be very alert, very
    > attentive, so that what we have seen and what we have learned doesn't become a
    > memory with which we look, and which is already a distortion. Look each time as
    > though it were the first time![12]

5. Examination of familiar working situations can reveal attitudes and
    relationships in a surprising new light.
        This principle counters the tendency to assume full knowledge of that
    which is already known to some degree. Those who take a suspicious second
    glance can be dismissed as time-wasters eager to reinvent the wheel.

    > Reinventing the wheel is not always the profitless exercise it is made out to be. Familiar
    > objects and ideas can be taken too much for granted: the wheel is just a wheel, and
    > one tends to stop thinking about it in terms of a relationship between a surface and
    > a vehicle. Conditions change, so that only through questioning that functional rela-
    > tionship does it become possible to confirm that the wheel really is the most appro-
    > priate solution. In this way better wheels are developed and very occasionally quite
    > new relationships are conceived; so the tank or the hovercraft gets invented.[13]

    The value of suspecting the apparent was validated by events in schools like
    Ryesdon, St Clare's with St Catherine's and Hill View, where examination of
    the taken-for-granted revealed splits in the staff groups and religious
    prejudice among the anti-racists.

6. Use of personal insights and resources in the professional context increases
    staff confidence, creativity and satisfaction.
        The majority of resources used by teachers in school are personal,
    connected with temperament, skill, experience or knowledge. Staff derive
    great satisfaction when elements of their wider life are helpful in broadening
    the professional expression of their colleagues. Making connections between

private enthusiasm and curriculum content, is affirming on every level and adds a creative spark to working life. RE development work is more likely to succeed when it confirms the constructive capacity of participants. The progress of work at George Street, St Clare's with St Catherine's and St Mark's was dependent on this type of energy.

7. Critical reflective work on the RE curriculum encourages mature dependence in working groups.

This principle emphasizes the development of trust between working colleagues. It protects the twin aspects of RE development, task and process, so that a working group will consciously reflect upon its own working styles and assumptions, checking for hidden agendas and anxieties which could be surfaced to enrich the work. This principle also stands for the spiral nature of any curriculum development and the requirement that policy and curriculum are subject to regular review.

8. Increasing staff competence in the management of ongoing experience and learning signals a change in school culture.

Every initiative has intended and unintended outcomes. In this instance RE work was the focus of the exercise. Since the work was also concerned with the acquisition of skills and perceptions, it had repercussions beyond that subject boundary.

This principle emphasizes the generic usefulness of consultancy-based RE curriculum development. St Benedict's used it to provide a general model of curriculum development. At St Clare's with St Catherine's and St Mark's, the headteachers saw it, in retrospect, as training for work on a school Mission Statement. In George Street, project experience brought about a conscious change in the management model of the school.

9. When staff have the courage to address the complexities of religion, history and culture they are freed to develop school policies directed towards the future.

This principle recognizes that RE development in the twentieth century is a complex and highly political activity. The case study material from Hill View, St Benedict's, Ryesdon and St Peter's throws light on the experience of those caught in the pinch of local, diocesan and national Church politics. RE renewal seems to involve risk.

> Risk brings its own rewards: the exhilaration of breaking through, of getting to the other side, the relief of a conflict healed, the clarity when a paradox dissolves . . . Eventually we know deeply that the other side of every fear is a freedom. Finally, we must take charge of the journey, urging ourselves past our own reluctance and misgivings and confusion to new freedom.[14]

10. RE renewal requires engagement and enlargement of the imagination.

Imagination gets a bad name when it is taken only to mean the exercise of fantasy to invent Never-Never Land. RE renewal requires vision. Those project schools which achieved few tangible results, St Peter's, Ryesdon and Hill View, were beset by either a crisis or failure of vision, an inability to relate the RE endeavour to contemporary life.

Powerful imagination is not false outward vision, but intense inward representation, and a creative energy constantly fed by susceptibility to the various minutiae of experience, which it reproduces and reconstructs, in fresh and fresh wholes; not the habitual confusion of provable fact with the fictions of fancy and transient inclination, but a breadth of ideal association which informs every material object, every incidental fact, with far reaching memories and stored residues of passion, bringing into new light the less obvious relations of human existence.[15]

These ten principles provide a framework for managing and evaluating RE development in the primary school.

Table 10.5 *Ten principles to put into practice*

1. Co-operative, collegial working styles generate a high degree of interest in and loyalty to the work in hand.

2. Development occurs when there is time and available energy for free-ranging and exploratory talk around the key issues.

3. Exploration of the feelings affecting the situation gives rise to new thoughts about it.

4. Professional learning takes place when a staff group can stay with the experience of 'not knowing', resisting a rush to quick solutions.

5. Examination of familiar working situations can reveal attitudes and relationships in a surprising new light.

6. Use of personal insights and resources in the professional context increases staff confidence, creativity and satisfaction.

7. Critical reflective work on the RE curriculum encourages mature dependence in working groups.

8. Increasing staff competence in the management of ongoing experience and learning signals a change in school culture.

9. When staff have the courage to address to complexities of religion, history and culture they are freed to develop school policies directed towards the future.

10. RE renewal requires engagement and enlargement of the imagination.

With RE inspection due to begin in 1994, there is an increasing interest in producing RE policy statements. Consideration of the pointers offered in this chapter would enable teachers to critique the factors which shape their own RE practice and aspirations. This may stimulate the imagination, which George Eliot celebrated as illuminative and able to disclose connections between different aspects of the world, and set a staff and school on a road to curricular critique and creativity.

NOTES AND REFERENCES

1. *First and Always*, edited by L. Snail (1988) (London: Faber & Faber), p. 34.
2. G. Eliot, *Daniel Deronda*, edited by B. Hardy (1986) (Harmondsworth: Penguin), p. 321.
3. M. Rossman (1973) *Learning Without a Teacher* (Bloomington, Indiana: Phi Delta Kappa), p. 28.
4. A. Ecclestone (1977) A *Staircase for Silence* (London: Darton, Longman & Todd), p. 36.
5. G. Eliot, *The Mill on the Floss*, edited by A. S. Byatt (1985) (Harmondsworth: Penguin), p. 628.
6. *Ibid.*

7. C. Castenada (1968) *The Teachings of Don Juan: A Yaqui Way of Knowledge* (New York: Ballantine), p. 326.
8. J. Bly (1992) *Iron John: A Book about Men* (Dorset: Element Books), pp. 174–5.
9. C. Rogers (1965) *Client-centred Therapy* (Boston: Houghton Mifflin), pp. 193–4.
10. J. Keats, *Letters of John Keats*, edited by R. Gittings (1987) (Oxford: OUP), pp. 249–50.
11. S. T. Coleridge, *Notebooks*, edited by K. Coburn (1957) (London: Routledge & Kegan Paul), Vol 3, No 3825.
12. J. Krishnamurti (1971) *The Flight of the Eagle* (New York: Harper & Row), p. 121.
13. E. J. Miller (1979) 'Open systems revisited: A proposition about development and change', in W. G. Lawrence (ed.), *Exploring Individual and Organizational Boundaries*, p. 217.
14. M. Ferguson (1980) *The Aquarian Conspiracy: Personal and Social Transformation in the Eighties* (Los Angeles: J. P. Tarcher), p. 294.
15. G. Eliot (1879), *Impressions of Theophrastus Such* (London: Cabinet Edition), p. 197.

Chapter 11

Postscript – To Create the World

> They, looking back, all th' eastern side beheld
> Of Paradise, so late their happy seat,
>
> Some natural tears they dropped, but wiped them soon;
> The world was all before them, where to choose
> Their place of rest, and Providence their guide:
> They hand in hand, with wand'ring steps and slow,
> Through Eden took their solitary way.
>
> *Milton, Paradise Lost, Book 12, lines 643–9*

Loss of a naive world view can be felt as paradise lost, albeit a fools' paradise lost. But self-knowledge and awareness of others confers a perspective on life which emphasizes dignity and responsibility. Like Milton's Adam and Eve, humanity takes tentative steps into the world, as its second creators. The greatest act of creation is to strive with others to be more fully human.

The present school curriculum prepares the next generation to incarnate this struggle at a time when newspapers and nightly newscasts proclaim a catalogue of worldwide inhumanity. Genocide, ethnic cleansing, inter-religious rivalries, discrimination, assassinations, repatriations and border disputes hammer home the message that to be different is to be dangerous, and in danger. This bad news raises questions about the individual's ability to tolerate those described as different. It appears to argue for bland similarity and repression of personal minority aspects as the only guarantee of survival.

We are not very different from each other biologically or physiologically. It is our different life stories which identify each one of us as unique. Being and becoming is about the possession, recollection and reconstruction of these inner narratives which claim particular racial, religious, cultural, political, moral and spiritual commitment.

Primary RE misses the mark if it fails to celebrate the inner worlds and particular faith stories that shape the different identities of pupils. It also falls short unless it prepares pupils to cope with the variety of stories, ideologies and commitments which compete to explain and determine how we live.

The cost of preserving a simple unified inner world is paid by those scapegoated to carry the ambiguities and unacknowledged differences of others into the spotlight of violent world conflict. Religious Education functions on the boundary where the inner world erupts into social expression. Those who work on this boundary, both pupils and teachers, are promoting care and reason in what may seem an unreasonable world. Their success will be prefigured by the extent to which they can understand and manage the effects of their own inner worlds on the wider social arena of classroom and staffroom.

Name Index

Agyris, C. 95
Anzieu, Didier 98
Arnold, Matthew 93
Atwood, Margaret 78

Bateson, Gregory 111
Bernstein, Leonard 68
Berry, Wendell 85
Beyer, L. 7
Bion, William 38–42, 49, 65, 75, 99
Bond, Edward 87, 94
Brecht, Bertold 76
Buber, M. 14

Campbell, Joseph 112
Cassian, Nina 35, 61
Castenada, Carlos 122
Cleese, John 10
Coleridge, Samuel Taylor 69
Crites, Stephen 110–11

Darwin, Charles 57
Dickinson, Emily 12
Durkheim, E. 13

Eisner, Elliot 10
Eliot, George 117, 130
Eliot, T.S. 94, 121

Fainlight, Ruth 73
Freud, Sigmund 37
Fromm, Eric 10
Frost, Robert 54

Gilbert, A.D. 15
Graves, Robert 22, 98

Holt, John 29
Hulmes, Edward 17

Islam, Yusuf 105

Jennings, Elizabeth 117

Kavanagh, Patrick 69, 108
Keats, John 68

May, Rollo 111
Menzies, Isabel 43
Milton, John 132

O'Keefe, Bernadette 61

Pascall, David 17–18
Patton, John vii-viii

Rice, Ken 77
Rich, Adrienne 60–1, 107
Rioch, Margaret 42
Rogers, Carl 124
Rossman, Michael 118
Rushdie, Salman 18, 69, 103, 111

Sarton, May 85, 97
Schon, D. 95
Shakespeare, William 51
Sisson, C.H. 83
Smith, Stevie 100–1
Sondheim, Stephen 113–14
Sorenson, Charles 106
Stenhouse, Laurence 26

Taylor, W. 26
Tebbit, Norman 7
Thomas, Dylan 47–8

White, J. 8
Williams, William Carlos 98
Witkin, F. 25

Subject Index

*(Where numerals are in **bold face**, this represents a subject covered by a chapter or section.)*

admissions policy, schools 52
agencies, influences of external 28–9, 30, 58
AIDS 52
aims, lack of clarity about 26–7, 30, 58
analysis, cultural 28–9, 58

answer-centredness 29
answers, importance of right 29, 45
anti-racism 123
anxiety
    Bion and 38
    defences against 36–8, 42–3
arson attack 101

Assessment Tests 16
Attainment Targets (ATs) 15–17, 26, 30
authority, teacher's 95

Basic Assumption Behaviour 39, 41–2, 44, 49, 65–7, 68, 76